D1557984

REFLECTIONS OF MY HIGHER SELF

A JOURNEY THROUGH IDENTITY, BELIEF, AND
PERCEPTION

JOSEPH DANNA

GOLDEN KEY PUBLISHING, AMHERST, NEW HAMPSHIRE

CONTENTS

Reflections of My Higher Self: *A Journey Through Identity, Belief, and Perception*

Edited by Cedar Trees Publishers
Formatted by Cedar Trees Publishers

Published by Golden Key Publishing
Amherst, New Hampshire

ISBN 9780692922132
ISBN-13: 978-0-692-92213-2

THANKS AND PERMISSION

The Rosicrucian Order, AMORC
www.rosicrucian.org

The Rosicrucian Code of Life (Le Tremblay: AMORC, 2005), 49. ©
2005 Supreme Grand Lodge of AMORC.
All rights reserved.

Teri Rider, Top Reads Publishing, Inc. for her consultation and
coaching skills.
www.teririder.com

The City of Gloucester, Massachusetts

Special thanks to Gail Mountain for her time and expert advice. I
hope I used it well. RIP, dear lady.

ACKNOWLEDGEMENTS

The Conquest of Frustration, Maxwell Maltz, Raymond Charles Barker, Ballantine Books, 1969

Seth Speaks, The Eternal Validity of the Soul, Jane Roberts 1972, Amber-Allen Pub. 1995-97

What You Think of Me is None of My Business, Terry Cole-Whittaker, Jove Publishing, 1981

A Course in Miracles, Foundation for Inner Peace, 1975

The Door of Everything, Ruby Nelson, DeVorss Publications, 1963

The Kybalion of The Three Initiates, BN Publishing, 2008

Escaping Christianity: Finding Christ, Barbara Symons, 2014

The Power of Now, Eckhart Tolle, 2010

The Self-Realization Fellowship, Los Angeles & Encinitas, Ca.

DEDICATION

To my Mother, Mary; to my Father, Phillip, may you RIP; to my sisters, Phyllis and Josie, and to the rest of my family.

To my cousin, Neil, gone too soon.

To Soror Rosalind Henning, a beloved Rosicrucian in transition.

To Gloria Avila, a guidepost on the path of so many. I love you. You are deeply missed.

To my beloved friend, David Barry, who made his transition shortly before this book went to print. You were a true friend. I can't believe you're gone. I'll never forget the "Little Piggies".

To my departed lifelong friend, Diane MacDonald. Remember "Old Friends, Bookends" was all about us.

To you, Jackie, who never failed to make me laugh. I love and miss you. RIP.

To Alfred, Rozzi, Cosmo, Teri, Anne, Manny, Donnie, Gail, Minky, Kendra, Peter Paul, Steve, Crissy, and my many other friends, who are gone way too soon.

The Landry family.

To anyone I have ever hurt.

NOTE

Not everything written in this book is necessarily a direct reflection of the philosophies or practices of any of the people, places, or organizations mentioned. As with any writing, whether old or new, this saying holds true: *Take from it what serves you and leave the rest.*

QUOTE

"…Most of us are intrigued by tales of adventure into other worlds. There is a thrilling romance in journeys across seas, over mountains and desert wastes, to remote places. In addition, by means of giant telescopes, astronomers today are probing worlds, which lie thousands of light years away in the vast reaches of outer space."

"Also, through electronic devices, modern physicists are exploring whole galaxies of energy, universes so infinitesimally small that they may be placed upon the head of a pin. And yet, for all this adventuring, there is still a realm into which most men have never entered. It is a strange region to them. Even their imaginations have never ventured to its frontiers or dared to cross its boundaries. It is the *world of self*. Unfortunately, to the majority of people, it constitutes an iron curtain behind which most men will not penetrate…"

FOREWORD

Given retrospectively through the character of Salvatore DiSanti, this universally themed fiction is set to a backdrop of real events in the author's lifetime.

The transmission considers different levels of receptivity in its audience; therefore, the expression of the same ideas from different angles may be repetitive to some, yet necessary to the assimilation of others who are unfamiliar with the material.

Please be assured that references to the harmful conveyances of authority figures and belief systems aren't made with the intent to place blame. Depictions of unfortunate events related to persons and religions are presented in the light that people often act without questioning the dominant forces in their lives.

Forgiveness is examined with the acknowledgment that it can sometimes be difficult, and at times impossible to give. The intention is to bring this difficulty into the light of a broader perspective, where the potential to see beyond our perceived capabilities waits to be recognized. The aim is to bring clarity to the truth that, nothing seen as external changes, until change occurs within us. Only then, can we begin to understand why we are better off not to freeze-frame ourselves in the past with an attitude of resentment.

To avoid confusion, I will take this time to say that Salvatore's inter-dimensional journey, the one which begins on the first stair-well landing of the Victorian he calls home in Chapter Ten, continues to take place on the stairwell through Chapter Twenty-Two.

NOTE

Before Creation, there was only the ONE LIGHT incorruptible. The Singular Universal Intelligence. No here and no there, no separation at all, for that would be Two. Yet without Two, the ONE couldn't be known, even unto Itself.

In Creation, ONE extended to Two in order to comprehend Itself through a counterpart; for a natural contrast of darkness occurred with the Two away from its home.

We are the Two… yet awakening to the ONE we are.

But the Law of the Triangle says a third part is necessary for completion. The Three is the realization of love, which runs through The ONE and The Two. Without it, you have not yet seen.

THE OLD NEIGHBORHOOD

"Living in the world without insight into the hidden laws of nature is like not knowing the language of the country in which one was born."

— Hazrat Inayat Khan

I held my vigil nightly while sitting on the top step in the hallway. The window I faced was four-square feet, and had a perimeter of stained-glass panes. I sat up there quietly, hidden in the dark, but the silence held no secrets when the nickel I dropped careened down the staircase like a tap dancer in an unforgiving library. Then I heard the sound of my mother's voice.

"Salvatore! What are you doing out there?"

"Nothin'," I replied innocently.

"Jesus, Phil— will you tell him to go to bed before he falls down the stairs? After all, he *is* only five years old and it's almost nine o'clock! For God's sake, do something, will ya?"

Mary DiSanti was my mother—a stout woman of power who got Dad's attention when she spoke.

"How many times do I have to tell him before he listens?" Dad asked. "What the hell is he doing out there, anyway?"

My father, Phillip DiSanti, was a fisherman who told many a tale about his adventures at sea, and we breathed in every word he uttered. I remember one story he told about being the watchman on deck one night, after they'd had a good catch. He said that as the boat clipped toward the Cape Cod Canal on its way to port, he slipped from the bow and fell overboard. Since he'd been alone on deck, he knew that the likelihood of being reported missing any time soon was close to zero, so his survival was solely up to him. Weighed down by heavy gear, including knee-high rubber boots, he summoned every ounce of strength in his body, and swam for his life towards the last of six bumper tires hanging starboard by a rope near the stern. As he got closer, he reached out and, barely grasping the tire, he hoisted himself back onto the boat. He thought it was only by the grace of St. Peter, the patron saint of fishermen, that he managed to save himself. My father made us laugh every time he raised his hands to his head and shrieked as he imitated the captain's outrage at his sopping state.

In another eerie story, Dad told of a time when he and the boat's crew were in Cape May, N.J. Since he was an experienced horseman, he decided to go riding with some of the other fishermen he had met there. After riding the trails, they were on their way back to the barn when they came upon a wooden bridge spanning a stream. The next thing my father knew, he was seven miles out to sea with no memory of crossing the bridge, returning the horse, or that he'd even gotten back on the boat. After figuring there were approximately four hours of time missing from his life, he kept the enigma to himself. The fishermen who had gone horseback riding with him were from other ports, and so he never saw them again. There were no reports of a fisherman's disappearance and rescue at sea, and there were no hints from anyone that anything unusual had happened. And that's the way dad left it.

My father never understood what happened to his four hours of missing time, and just like him, neither would I understand some of the mysterious experiences waiting to occur in my future.

My mother nagged Dad about my being up too late, so he followed through with his nightly routine. I liked being carried, so when Dad came to retrieve me from the top step in the hallway, I feigned sleep in order to get a ride up to bed. But there was no way I could ever stay there. Sneaking around corners to return to my perch on the stairway was easy, and within minutes, I was in the hallway again, monitoring the window below, waiting, just waiting.

The Indian in full headdress didn't come every night, but that night he showed. Whether or not he floated above the ground or was simply ten feet tall, I don't know, but the upper part of his body, from below his shoulders to just above his head, filled up the high window as he passed by like a magnetic wave. As always, he approached from the right, so initially I only saw his left profile. But when he got to the middle of the window, he turned to face me with his hand raised in some unfamiliar gesture. His face seemed to radiate its own light; his presence permeated every particle of my being, and his gleaming eyes brought all my senses to life. Then he turned again and continue on his way. Instead of being afraid, I welcomed and loved the energized sensations he evoked in me!

After that night, my Indian never appeared in the window again. He was gone for now.

Sometimes I tried to tell my parents why I liked being in the hallway, but before I could finish, they dismissed my explanations as a child's imagination, bringing the discussion to an abrupt end. Were they so frightened of the unknown that they evaded investigating these kinds of oddities?

Too young to know much about Native Americans at the time, it was much later that I related the many feathers of his headdress to those of a Chief, and his hand gesture to some kind of *mudra*.

Years later, there was talk that the whole neighborhood was haunted. I once heard my dad say that the previous occupants of our home had claimed that ghosts had walked freely all throughout the house. They'd been so afraid that they finally ran off into the night, never to return. As I listened to that story, an inner sense told me that I'd eventually come to learn that the word *ghost* was far from a definition for my Indian, and that he would return to me at the appropriate time and place in my life.

Slowly, but surely, I was growing up, and in September of 1959, I began school. I choked back tears when my mother left me in the classroom for the first time. But I wasn't upset for long, because just as my sister had assured me, first grade was about ringing bells, singing songs, and coloring books.

Mrs. Hinckley was my teacher. She had a knack for keeping the class interested in the basics, like reading and writing. I loved her. But the succeeding years stood in stark contrast to that initial ease. Most teachers in the subsequent grades were formidable, to say the least. In the early 1960s, some of them used corporal punishment as a vehicle to vent their anger and frustrations.

To this day, it's still unsettling when I recall the disciplinary actions my second and third grade teacher took when her demands weren't met. She terrified me. *Spare the rod, spoil the child* was the law of the times—a law she wasted no time abusing. While under her wrath for two successive years, I often looked out the window, immersed in daydreams. She dutifully noted my absentmindedness on every failing report card. I became increasingly withdrawn. Although I told my parents about the behavior of this beast of a teacher, they never explored the option for me to leave her class. The thought had never occurred to me that it was even possible. That was just the way it was back then.

In elementary school, I religiously looked forward to three

o'clock when class was dismissed for the day, and I could run home to drain every last drop of affection from my big Sicilian grandmother until she yelled up the stairs in broken English for my mother to come and get me.

I drove my grandmother crazy because I couldn't get enough of her, or the fragrance of her apartment, and the idea that there might be hidden treasures in the deep recesses of her china closet. How could I think otherwise, since it once birthed a Davy Crockett jackknife and a box of chocolate-covered cherries? I loved my grandmother more than words could say, even more than the yellow cream cannolis hidden in her refrigerator.

Those times of my young life are etched in my mind, never to be forgotten.

My name is Salvatore DiSanti, and I grew up by the sea. The New England port I called home provided a neighborhood that was every kid's dream. We had assigned names for every area of its two blocks that were divided by Locust Street. One was called *Big Block* and the other *Little Block*.

There was the gabled *Fitz Hugh Lane House,* made of granite blocks and known by the old-timers as *The Stone Jug* because it once served as a jail for unruly mariners. *Big Rock* was, well, a large granite rock I used to rest upon. It lay hidden on a slope adjacent to the *Fitz Hugh Lane House;* it's also where the bells in the carillon of *Our Lady of Good Voyage Church* lulled me to heavenly states on Sundays. The rock still sits behind a building across the street from Captain Carlo's Restaurant.

As far as we kids were concerned, Duncan Street was lined with haunted houses. An old fish-processing plant that had seen its time stood there, too. There were no floors in this huge, burned-out brick building that had a thick rope hanging from a beam in the middle of its high ceiling. With the rope in hand, we'd scale fifty feet of its inner wall up to a ledge, and then jump while bellowing our Tarzan calls across its great length. It was a dangerous swoop, but we didn't care. We were fearless kids, who swan-dived from high up on the masts of fishing boats.

An industrious fish town, it offered something new to explore with every passing season. The salty breezes from the North Atlantic, and a range of unsavory aromas crisscrossed my stomping grounds: the stench of fish guts from the processing plants at low tide, the vapors of freshly painted trawlers, barnacle scrapings, and putty. The east side of the island offered panoramas, like *Good Harbor Beach* that transformed into an ocean mineral bath during the dog days of August.

That was Cape Ann, and all who lived there knew there was no other place like Gloucester, Massachusetts. I learned to swim off the piers in my town where seagull shit burned the paint from cars and promised good luck with a splat on the head.

As kids, we made racing cars out of broken shopping carts we found behind the local grocery store, devised our own version of skateboards, and played hide-and-go-seek on hot summer nights while eating the best pizza and frozen lemonade in town.

In winter, we rummaged through our cellars for sleds and ice-skated on flat rooftops. We suffered all the cuts, scrapes, stitches, and broken bones that an active childhood amid the docks, warehouses, and railways had to offer—all to a backdrop of lunchtime whistles blowing from the wharves.

When I was in the sixth grade, our teacher announced to the class that the neighborhood of slums on the waterfront was being taken over by Eminent Domain for Urban Renewal. Like my preceding teachers, Mrs. Carter was from the artsy east end of town, and spoke condescendingly about my little piece of heaven. With haughty eyes enhanced by perfectly applied mascara, she often scoffed at the locals when she sauntered around the cobblestone of Gloucester. It was clear that she didn't like us "half-breeds".

When I protested her rant about the government razing what

she referred to as "the dilapidated houses" on my street, she responded to my protests by wryly claiming that it was "necessary to beautify the city", and then commanded me to "STAND!"

She made a beeline toward the rear of the class, thrust her hand to my chest, and twisting my shirt, taking skin with it, she hoisted all sixty-eight pounds of me to my toes. With a grimace from hell, she challenged me in an ugly stare down, which of course she won. I was in shock, not understanding the affront, but knowing for sure that for some reason, the old wretch despised me.

Despite her untimely outbursts, Mrs. Carter, or Pauline to the other teachers was often described as "effervescent like a bottle of champagne" by some. One June day, she teased-up her red hair, donned a yellow dress and white open-toed shoes, and hit Main Street, Gloucester, for her morning walkabout. Looking like a lit-up Roman Candle in that T-shirt-jeans-and-pony-tail part of town, she almost caused an accident as drivers and pedestrians alike stopped to gaze at the peculiar sight.

My Virgo stomach had no tolerance for tomato sauce, so when my folks made me eat spaghetti and meatballs twice a week like clockwork, I puked all over the sidewalk in front of our house. On one of those days, I heard a cackle coming from the open window of a passing Cadillac, and I looked up to see Mrs. Carter behind the wheel with a look of disdain on her face. "There goes that Irish-Guinea again!" she cried, before driving off.

The brunt of Urban Renewal hit hard when we had to move. My neighborhood disappeared, house-by-house. Old ladies stood wailing while their dwellings were demolished, because that wasn't just *any* neighborhood. Those century-old houses had their own personalities, and the echo of gulls' calls was unique amongst them. The surrounding elm trees were their siblings, offering hiding places inside their split trunks, and giant mushrooms that my grandma used to sneak into her secret sauce.

During the onslaught, I checked daily to see if my house was still alive, but I couldn't bear to face what was in store, so I left it to my Dad. He described in detail how one corner of its foundation was gouged, and how our house at 125 Rogers Street was pushed by a bulldozer from the opposite side until it toppled. Then the same heavy equipment ran over, and flattened it—along with its stained-glass window, through which I had seen my Indian, and the hallway that echoed the laughter of so many cousins, aunts, and uncles. No longer would my grandmother sit in her place on the front porch, nor would she ever sweep the sidewalk again. Our house, its neighborhood, and everything about it was gone forever.

I was too young to understand the government and Eminent Domain. All I knew was that what they thought to be a bunch of old worn-down houses, was our place in the world, and was like sacred ground to us. For months into the aftermath of the destruction, the barren land they'd left was an assault to the senses. What happened was nothing less than an invasion that never really amounted to what I'd call progress. The road is a little wider, and there's a new police station next to a small plaza.

The Fitz Hugh Lane House, where my friends once lived and told stories of ghostly prisoners dragging chains through its supposed underground tunnels connected to the wharf, is now a museum. It still overlooks the harbor atop the hill once known as Ivy Court, where we rode our sleds in winter and our spirits danced upon the songs of a million starlings in summer. They should have left us natives alone, and told the tourists and the arty-fartys headed east on Coastal Route 127 to take the damn highway.

Urban renewal, slums… Bah! Those houses were so sturdy, they had a hard time knocking them down, and double for the trees. They withstood many a nor'easter that would reduce most of today's flimsy constructs to tumbleweed.

2

THE SEARCHLIGHT OF
INTROSPECTION

"I am not bound to win, but I am bound to be true. I am not bound to succeed, but I am bound to live up to what light I have."

— Abraham Lincoln

I knew we'd survive when my parents bought a house farther to the west side of town near a vista of marshlands that lay before the Annisquam River, and led to the drawbridge that opened to Gloucester Harbor. The property was rundown, but we liked the idea that it was so big, we got lost inside. It had a huge sunny yard to the delight of green thumbs, so its condition didn't matter much to us. Aunts, uncles, cousins, and friends converged like worker bees to scrape, paint, and hang wallpaper, while carpenters tore down old walls, replaced staircases, and fitted ceramic tiles. We relished the smell of newness without saying.

Due to distance, friendships from the old neighborhood dwindled, so the local kids had to make suitable, new comrades.

I'd hated school since the second grade, so transferring to a new one was uncomfortable, at best. Due to past experience with teachers, adult authority figures made me apprehensive. In the grips of an overwhelming sense of inferiority, standing in line at the new school was a form of unspoken torture.

Through the windows of the lobby, the teachers monitored the courtyard where we stood, while inside my head, I envisioned the ground swallowing me, removing me from the pressure of their stares. One of my new teachers glared at me regularly, which fed my insecurity and left me to the mercilessness of a fight-or-flight quandary. As I sat in the classroom feeling like a trapped animal, fear grew in me, and I didn't know why. Aside from the harsh treatment I'd gotten from school teachers, I'd always sensed there was a deeper underlying cause for the discomfort affecting my young life. I just didn't know what it was. All I knew was that, for the time, I longed for summer, just so I could get away from school.

Summer came at last, and my red bike with the high handlebars made it easy to spend most of my time across the river in my cousin's neighborhood. Neil was a joke machine, and good at sports. We spent our days playing football, fishing for striped bass, and gambling for quarters.

The year 1966 was unique. The air was filled with magic. The Beatles, and a slew of other musical groups ruled the airwaves, as Janis Joplin, Jimi Hendrix, and The Doors waited to erupt from the wings. We milked that summer for all its worth, then fall arrived, too soon, just like it always did in New England. Once again, it was time for new clothes, curfews, alarm clocks, and now grammar school.

With its three stories of old brick and squeaky hardwood floors that told of previous generations, the seventh grade presented yet another school akin to a penitentiary. There were a few great teachers, but there were also others who were demented, and ruled with iron fists.

Induced by the aroma of freshly baked buns wafting from the

cafeteria, the comfort of home was oddly interwoven with the fear of knowing you would probably get into a fight after the lunch bell rang. We had to learn how to scrap in this school, lest we be trampled underfoot.

The YMCA dances on Friday nights were the way to go, and a six-pack of beer was sufficient for three. In those days, I was like a walking sensitivity meter. All of my senses were so activated and entangled that it made my life either uncomfortable, or beautifully wondrous, depending on the situation. I felt everything, even the smell of a new record added to the musical experience.

Winter gave way to spring, and the wonderment of being all of fifteen years old ruled the summer. I couldn't be separated from my growing group of pals and our revelry in finding hidden nooks to drink and play cards on weekends. Those were our glory days, when feeling good and knowing the right people were all that mattered—or so we thought.

The rapid cultural change of the 1960s and 70s was reflected in the dress code of my high school. During my freshman year in 1967, guys had to wear neckties, sports coats, dress pants, and loafers and, were required to crop their hair above the ear in what was called a "Regular" man's haircut. By 1971, we tossed our ties and wore everything from cowboy boots and fringed suede jackets, to jeans and shorts, while smoking cigarettes in the schoolyard with hair curling down our backs.

The whims of the younger generation and those simple manifestations symbolized a change in thinking—a questioning of perception—which, for many of us, went beyond our rebellion against society's norms to a deepening curiosity about *the workings of perception itself.* As Viet Nam exploded in our faces day and night on TV, my thoughts evolved from dress codes, and I began to question the reasoning behind countless wars throughout history. Casualties of this war reached all the way to our little town, and my generation was next in line to head for Southeast Asia. It hit home. I could only ask, *Why do we, as the human race, as a species, think the way we do? Why are we killing each other?* Thankfully, the draft system changed and I wasn't forced to go to war.

Questions like these led me to look within at my own manner of thinking. They opened a pathway of soul-searching in me, not only because of endless strife in the world, but because I had my own personal thorns screaming for attention. The discomfort I'd felt since elementary school had grown to serious bouts with anxiety to the point where it was time to see a doctor.

A caring nurse at the medical facility asked me if I meditated. I told her that I was raised Catholic and didn't know much about meditation, but that I prayed often. I thought back to earlier years, and how I had difficulty understanding what I'd heard in church and what was taught in Sunday school. I recalled how I viewed priests and nuns as far superior to me. So, if they said I was bad, I'd feel worse than bad. A lingering uncertainty about whether I was going to heaven or hell was like a haunt that followed me through my teens.

I began to question authority. Who were these people, or any people, who were somehow in charge of what I was supposed to think and feel? These were concepts I needed to understand. I was far too frustrated for a seventeen-year-old. One day, a book titled, *The Conquest of Frustration,* jumped out at me from a book rack. This was the first book that led me to explore the laws of perception and the crossroads of psychology with spirituality. What I learned certainly helped, but my questions about the workings of life seemed unending.

Developing the sense that strength born of knowledge was inspired by the willingness to overcome the discomfort of ignorance, I never gave up on my search for a greater truth in life than what I'd found in religion. I looked everywhere, except for where it lay. Now and then, I was pointed in what seemed the right direction, but ultimately, I couldn't connect with what was presented.

Various philosophies were inspiring in concept, yet I wasn't experiencing their truth.

A discussion group would have been ideal, but in the early 1970s, there weren't a lot of visible people around my neck of the woods who were talking about the mysteries of the universe. According to my friends' parents, the best thing anyone could do to enrich his or her life was to land a relatively high-paying job at the seafood processing plant atop the hill downtown. In other words, I had no cohorts to help reinforce the part of my psyche that wanted to grow.

In regard to my new interest in the workings of perception, my first close look at the idea that everyone was unique and saw things only according to what was in their own head, had me feeling a strange sense of abandonment. I wasn't used to thinking in this new way. I was, in fact, quite alone with it, which only served to make it more disorienting. Was I just growing up and withdrawing from tribal thinking, or was I thinking too much and stunting my growth? Unbeknownst to me at the time, my sense of identity was beginning to be shaken to the core; and it needed to be.

The process of examining thought patterns pertaining to personal identity was unsettling, and it left me rustling through pages of books in hopes of finding kinship with silent voices in the night. The idea of people's differing perspectives came to me symbolically. I had inner visions of rays of light projecting from different angles through human filters of belief. In turn, these beliefs formulated every individual's personal movie on the screens of their respective lives. But from where was I looking? When examining my own perspective, I realized that I had gained a new ability to put aside what beliefs I held, simply because I understood the dynamic of belief and how it worked to create everyone's separate movie. Beliefs, along with the stream of thoughts and emotions attached to them, were beginning to be regarded as secondary to something deeper concerning my identity.

I found myself looking at life from an *in-between-my-thoughts* kind of place. So, what was my identity without beliefs, without conditioning? Was I making myself crazy? I struggled to grasp the magnitude of what now seemed like an involuntary process. No one I knew could understand what was happening with me. Any mention of it either raised eyebrows or prompted people to tell me to *Stop reading those books!* A friend of my parents cornered me one day, and asked, "What's wrong with you? Are you on drugs?"

Being a pioneer in my thinking had a liberating aspect, but it was also daunting. I didn't know how to ground myself with a strong sense of identity. I was still a follower who needed people when the drug invasion of early 1970s Gloucester affected me. Although I wasn't around drugs long enough for them to steal my life, I did self-medicate to get temporary relief from the emotional storm churning within. As is always the case with substance abusers, drugs weren't my primary problem. My issue was more about dealing with an identity crisis completely on my own.

Going through puberty as a teenager with accelerated hormones was no easy task. What made it more difficult for me, was that for some unknown reason, I had an inferiority complex. A bad word directed at me could be debilitating. The full realization that the thoughts of others were none of my business, was yet to be. Strength born of knowledge hadn't yet taken root and grown, and in its place were feelings of separation.

I didn't know it at the time, but I was suffering from the cumulative effects surrounding an incident which occurred earlier in my childhood. Years later, this would be revealed to me in an unbelievable and extraordinary way.

As the nurse's question about meditation lay heavy on my mind, an inner force pushed me to become deeply contemplative in regard to where I fit in with God. I still wasn't quite sure. I'd heard so many things about the topic. Then once again, I stumbled upon an *opening* between my thoughts. It was an opening to an expanded sense of my being involving random clairvoyance and peculiar events—the first of which was related to the death of a friend.

3

A WAY OF SEEING

"We can easily forgive a child who is afraid of the dark; the real tragedy of life is when men are afraid of the light."

— Plato

In August of 1974, at twenty years of age, I awoke one night, feeling like I'd just returned from hanging off the edge of a cliff. While sitting on my bed at three o'clock in the morning, and considering the freshness of my recall, there was no doubt in my mind that I'd just had an out-of-body experience. Having a strong practical side, I looked for ways to rationalize other people's claims of extrasensory perceptions, and approached what I thought might be my own, even more stringently.

Unaware of any psychic-type predisposition before that night, I believe I stepped from the sleep state into another sphere that opened to the onset and completion of my friend Alberto's departure from this world.

I saw what I referred to as energetic swirls in the air that I didn't understand in this strange 'other' place. There was a grayish tint in the air, sort of like fog, and other beings were present to escort my friend, who was reluctant to go, and who was so full of resistance, he might as well have been standing in front of a speeding train.

Although our bodies looked different from the norm, we recognized each other. With a look of desperation, he reached for me, and we went through the motions of latching hand-to-wrist in a fireman's grip; however, we never made physical contact because our bodies were made of a finer substance, not flesh and blood like in the physical realm.

My sudden entrance into the momentum of this process prohibited any thought of questioning the situation. All I felt was an intense, emotional upset, and I acted instinctively by trying to help my friend. The other beings present were assisting with his crossover in some manner I couldn't understand. When they noticed my presence and acknowledged it to each other, I got the feeling that I had somehow slipped through the cracks that led me to this place.

In the continuity of what I interpreted as an *axis-shift* set to a specific velocity throughout the event, he became a liquefied magnet. I watched helplessly as his form elongated and slipped away like an electrical fluidity disappearing through a point in space.

Bolting straight up in bed and soaked in sweat with my heart pounding, I shouted his name, "AL!" Too shaken by the abruptness of my return at the precise moment he'd slipped away, and too infused with his fearful unwillingness to depart, I did not sleep for the rest of the night.

I had no doubt that the phone would ring with bad news in the hours to come. When it did, I stood at the top of the stairs waiting to hear my mother's voice. I mouthed the words as she cried, "Your friend Alberto died last night!"

He was actually killed in a drug-related incident. The word

was out that someone had purposely overdosed him with heroin. My intense feeling about his vehement resistance to cross over was that at only twenty-five years old, he did not want to die because he knew the devastating effect it would have on his family. He felt as if his transition was an unwelcome ripping away from everything he knew and loved. I felt it, too.

Alberto wasn't someone I saw every day and we weren't so close that we called to make plans, but we had known and liked each other for years. When I actually received the expected phone call in the morning, thoughts that I might have unconsciously fabricated the experience of the night flew out the window, along with skepticism of the unknown.

I paced anxiously that morning, exclaiming that I had just seen Alberto in my sleep. There was no other choice but for me to accept this occurrence, and to not be so bold as to say that I knew exactly what it was, or why I was there. As I sat on the edge of my bed, something inside soothed me. It told me that Alberto was moved through his transition quickly, and was delivered to a place of serenity.

What happened in my sleep-state remained beyond the threshold of my understanding for decades. It was dissonant to my everyday life. Taking future advice from my mysterious friend, Michael, I placed all wonder about it aside for the day when I might fully know the workings of such things.

The clairvoyance that came with the *opening between my thoughts* was intermittent. It could occur once or twice a month, or once every few years. I could only surmise that my mind had the ability to become receptive in that way, but that I wasn't yet adept at adjusting some *inner antennae* necessary for fuller attunement.

In later years, while leaving for work at six o'clock one fall morning, another example of this sensory faculty became apparent to me. Not only did I *see* into my reception of an event, but I was also clairaudient, meaning, I *heard*. A sense of great urgency with people fleeing amid muffled screams entered my mind. All I could relate it to was the chaotic news clip I'd previously seen of the Hindenburg crash of 1937. So powerful was this episode, I pulled my car over to the side of the road. I felt that something big was happening, something that would be all over the network broadcasts, so I turned on my radio. However, I heard no unusual news, so I blew it off as some strange mental chatter.

It happened again the next day—still nothing on the radio, so I ignored it. There was a chaotic background of mental interference for much of the following day. I couldn't relate it to anything, so once again, I let it go. What else was I to do?

Rarely, did I watch television in the morning, but it was on the morning after those psychic disturbances that Diane Sawyer, host of *Good Morning America*, appeared on the screen with the news that there was an accident in New York City. It was assumed that a small plane had hit one of the Trade Towers, but it wasn't yet clear what happened, or why. Then, a few minutes later, I witnessed a jet airliner hit the other tower on live television, and the horror of that day unfolded right before my eyes. We were under attack!

I'll never know what might have come to mind had I gone to a quiet place to be still shortly before the events of 9-11 were broadcasted. Clairvoyance was still strange to me; my episodes had been camouflaged with remoteness. But the mental influxes I'd gotten in the days before 9-11 were so strong, I'd stopped my car on the side of the road. However, nothing had come with instructions, and there weren't any flashing signs of specificity.

4

MYSTERIOUS MICHAEL

"No act of kindness, no matter how small, is ever wasted."

— Aesop

During a walk on the beach one night, my friend, Michael, told me that I was overly empathetic. He explained that without realizing it, I left myself wide open to the emotional energies of others and everything around me. According to him, I was like a photographic plate waiting to be imposed upon in both the event with Alberto, and the terrorist attack twenty-seven years later.

He said that during his transition, Alberto telepathically contacted me through the desperation of his emotion. He added that the horror of September 11th crossed time, and because of the magnitude of its breadth, it imprinted onto my consciousness to some degree. He didn't mean that the ability to receive these transmissions was bad, just that I didn't understand what was happening.

"You need to understand why you are so susceptible to these

energies, and then learn what it means to protect yourself," Michael said.

I wasn't yet familiar with the natural laws of the universe, so Michael's explanations of how energy worked fell mostly on deaf ears.

"Thought is electromagnetic energy and the emotions attached to it act as catalysts," he further explained. "Whatever someone is feeling has potential. You, Salvatore, have a tendency to walk right into other people's emotional energy with your guard down, and consequently, you take on their energy as if it were your own. There have been times when you've become so hooked up with the emotional tone of others, that it became a habit for them to draw on your energy. Even now, some of the people you hang with use you like food. Your naiveté about what's happening puts you at such a disadvantage."

"Do you think that was the case with my last roommates?" I asked. "I didn't feel right for a long time after they moved."

"I didn't want to say this, Salvatore, but to see you after they finally left your place was like looking at a shadow of your former self."

"Michael, what started as a helping hand evolved into an emotional dependency. I don't understand exactly how it happened, but before they came, I was feeling really good. By the time they left, I felt like I'd had a lobotomy." I equated how I felt during that time to someone pulling a rug out from under my feet. I'd been quite disturbed, even disoriented.

"All kidding aside, Salvatore, you stepped up to help, but you were foolish in thinking you could help resolve all their life-problems. In fact, there's a co-dependent dynamic at work in you, which lays the groundwork for disappointment in such circumstances. This dynamic says, you shouldn't be happy, unless everyone around you is happy."

Michael paused and reached for his cigarettes. He lit one up, took a puff, and exhaled smoke into the night air. He shook his head, grimaced, and stared at the ground. "Those people had serious mental issues, far beyond what you were able to deal with. I don't know how to say..." He shrugged, raised his head and looked me square in the eyes. "I mean, you know, I love you to death, Salvatore, and wouldn't say anything to intentionally hurt you, but how other people feel is not your responsibility. Yet, you opened your home to them, placed yourself directly in line with their energy, and put up with all their chaos. The difference in you before they came and after they left was clear evidence of what happens when disharmonic energies are paralleled. Negativity from their end was so strong that it affected you by pulling on your vibration over a long period of time. That wouldn't have happened, *unless you felt there was something you wanted or needed from them.* It takes at least two, kid, and your supposed generosity at the time developed into a train wreck that gave birth to a three-headed monster. They and you."

Michael, a right-brained artistic intellectual, and my new best friend, was twenty-seven-years-old, like me. He could explain almost anything from societal woes to the mysteries of the universe while drawing the wind with the point of a pencil. At over six-feet-tall and weighing about two-hundred and thirty-pounds, he wore vivid tie-dyed shirts, and had a powerful voice that could scare strangers away.

We walked the beach on that September night to the distant whir of machinery, our hair and clothes permeated with the briny odor of whatever the barge offshore dredged on a continual basis. The pump-laden barge was part of a state-funded project designed to stop coastal erosion by redirecting sand two miles away to the southern area of the beach via an eighteen-inch diameter pipe.

It may sound odd, but Michael was a friend I could go to when I wanted to be alone, but didn't want to be by myself. We strode alongside the clattering pipe, making our way toward the end while voicing our growing curiosity at what flowed inside.

"Mostly rocks, I'm sure," Michael grumbled.

For some reason, a fleeting thought had me wondering if the adjacent river that flowed into the sea might have carried something more interesting from the lowlands and deposited it offshore to where it would be dredged. I began thinking about a recent discovery that claimed the lowlands were the grounds of an ancient Native American settlement. The thought dissipated when Michael interrupted, and proceeded to state exactly what he felt about another interpersonal scenario he had witnessed in my life.

"Alright, Salvatore. Do you remember when you took care of… I can never remember his name. What was it, Don?"

"Yeah, Don. How could I ever forget?"

"Well, that situation was spawned in hell, too."

"Michael, he was terminally ill. What was I supposed to do? There was no one else available to care for him," I explained, in an attempt to be understood.

"I know he was sick, but he was going through your mail and abusing you in all sorts of ways for the year you lived with him, never paying you a penny when he had millions. When he was well, and you worked for his business, he drove you into the ground with eighty-hour workweeks, and manipulated you as though you were an extension of him," Michael declared, flailing his hands in the air.

"There were unforeseen circumstances in his business. In later years, when he became ill and asked if I'd stay to help him, I couldn't just say no."

"Well, before he got ill, when you were homeless because of your back injury, being down on your luck or whatever… It makes no difference… He laughed at you and called you a bum. That alone should have been enough for you to sever all ties with him.

Why did you stay? Did you think he was going to leave you money or something?" Michael appeared both sympathetic and incensed.

"Listen, man, when I asked myself the same question about his money, my answer was that even if he was broke, I would have been there to help him because he was desperate."

"You could have left when he crossed every personal boundary known to man. That's what it was, you know. You had no sense of personal boundaries, at all. You still don't. Even after he held you like a prisoner in his house and demanded constant attention, you still felt guilty when you finally exploded and left."

"I did what I thought was the right thing because I liked Don. There were good times, too, you know. Everyone involved knew he was a control freak, but I put that aside, thinking it would be a thing of the past because he was so ill," I said, in a futile solicitation of Michael's good graces. "Leaving my own apartment to move in with him was a mistake, but he cried for me to stay. All in all, my initial response to be of assistance wound up to be a form of misplaced compassion. I became exasperated because I was unaware of just how much stress an incredibly demanding person could generate under such extenuating circumstances. Jesus, Michael, give me a break, will you?"

As irritation from the experience built up inside me, I extended my head backward to relieve the tension from the front of my neck. Then, I slowly flexed it forward, bringing my chin to my chest while forcefully dragging both hands from my forehead to the back of my skull in an effort to remove the mental poison of the past from my brain.

"Salvatore, have you ever considered that no one can be controlling unless there are other people around who are allowing themselves to be controlled?" Michael asked, in a calm voice.

"That sounds very obvious, but for some reason I hadn't thought about it that way. I just wanted to be of help."

"Of course, it's good to help others, but you can't help others until you help yourself, and that's what you fail to do. You seem to carry this inborn guilt, as if you're indebted to people. I don't know why you do that, but it doesn't do you any good."

I couldn't tell if Michael's half smile meant that he had a glimmer of hope that I'd rectify his self-destructive summation of my personality, or if he felt embarrassed for me.

"You need to look within yourself to see where the guilt is coming from. The only thing this allowance for abuse does is diminish you. Turn around for a second, Salvatore."

"Why?" I asked with a skeptical frown.

He laughed, and said, "I just want to check your back for a sign that says, *Doormat!*"

"Aw, hush, Michael." I chuckled in spite of the admonition he'd been doling out.

Michael eased up a bit as he looked north to where the river flowed into the ocean. Then all of a sudden, he began talking about Native Americans who once lived upstream in centuries past, and how he always imagined discovering relics while sifting through the grit as it exited the pipe's outlet further south on the beach.

While listening to him, I remembered something that happened earlier, right after we'd shared our curiosities of what might be in the pipe: As we'd fallen into silence, I recalled the recent discovery that the lowlands were once a Native American settlement and I was imagining finding something interesting in the sludge dredged from offshore, when Michael abruptly inter-rupted my thoughts by forcing a new topic of discussion. I wondered now if he'd read my mind then, and had intentionally changed the focus of my thoughts only to revisit the subject at his discretion? And why now? What was the significance of addressing the topic at this precise moment? I felt as if he was playing some kind of mind game with me, especially as it became increasingly difficult to ignore the fact that he often had a look on his face that said he knew something that I didn't. No doubt I seemed perplexed to him.

He appeared to sigh apologetically, then raised his hands toward the night sky and intoned one long, "OM", as if to call upon the Gods.

As we stood at the pipe's outlet, Michael lay bare his treasure-hunting side and beamed with enthusiasm as the water and its contents gushed out. But nothing of any ancient civilization was yet to be found, just broken shrubs washed from the lowlands, into the sea, then pumped through the pipe and deposited onto the beach.

Michael tossed the spent cigarette he never finished smoking, then rushed to retrieve a spiny branch that shot out of the gushing pipe. Holding it up to the moonlight, he stood transfixed, and yelled, "What a haunting appearance! Notice how the branches reach out in one direction as though frozen in the wind," he added, with new life in his voice, and a look on his face that suggested creative visions were swimming through his head. He set the petrified mesquite aside to cart home later, then sat down beside me.

As I began wondering about his artistic intentions, he suddenly resumed probing into my life with annoying and even more discomforting questions.

"As I was saying, for you to stay in those types of situations, there must have been something you wanted from the people with whom you were involved, Salvatore. So, what was it? Did you need attention or some kind of validation? You really need to look at why you believe it's your responsibility to ensure that the lives of the people around you are in order, and that they are happy. I mean, to the extent that you do."

Michael spoke slowly and with precision, as though he pondered my plight against the checklist of some inner archive. I felt embarrassed while thinking about what he said. *What did I want?* Something told me I had been attempting to create an extended family with the people surrounding me. Other than that, I drew blanks, so I let it rest.

"Do you look for others to fill you? I'm not talking about the sharing of fun and all the things friendship brings. I'm asking if you need their stamp of approval before you can feel good about yourself and your actions?"

"Gosh, that sounds so early 1970s. But to be honest, I do, in a way." I shrugged and peered at him through puckered brows. "Doesn't everybody need some degree of approval from their friends?"

"Yeah, but I'm not talking about superficial acts that draw a "Yea" or a "Nay". I mean, *you*. Does the way you feel about *Salvatore* depend on them, or on you?"

Even though Michael spoke in careful tones, I wasn't sure I liked what I was hearing.

"I'm only asking because I've noticed that you have a tendency to feel a little too hurt when someone says something about you that you don't like," he said, pointedly.

"Wow! You're really on a roll tonight, aren't you? Let's pull up some driftwood and set a spell, have a knock-down-drag-out," I said in a tone nearing sarcasm. Okay, I was getting a little irate.

We paid little attention to the continuous pinging of small rocks, and the scraping sounds of branches as they struck the interior of the pipe, but then something coursing toward the outlet generated a comparatively louder thud that attracted Michael's attention and brought him to his knees in the silt.

"What is it?" I shouted as he pulled something from the sludge.

"Wait a minute," he growled in his scare-people-away voice. Carrying his mysterious find with him, he walked to the seawall about twenty feet behind us, and placed it in a sack with the rest of his collection.

"What did you find?" I yelled as he stared into the sack.

"It's nothing."

"I'm sorry. Come back and sit down," I called out, sensing displeasure in his gruff response.

He reluctantly retraced his steps to our spot, and then said in that gruff voice again, "There's nothing else to talk about, Salvatore."

"I just felt like you were going too fast," I said in an effort to appease his sudden, sullen mood. "You lost me. Some of the things you said seemed a bit offensive."

"Or maybe they got a little too close to the truth? I'm not going to talk about it anymore, right now. Once you get all defensive on your high horse, and cock your head the way you do, the conversation is over for me. I was walking on eggshells trying to get something through to you."

"Huh? Cock my head?"

"Yeah. There's a way you turn your head when you're pissed."

Michael cocked his head to the side, I guess in a manner to demonstrate. "When I see you do that, I know there's no use in talking to you."

"Are you for real? What the—"

"There you go again, Salvatore. Sheesh!"

I threw my hands in the air. "Alright, you win. If you think it's going to prevent impending train wrecks in my life, then just say what's on your mind. I'll let you talk. I promise to listen."

Michael took a deep breath, and in his unique manner, he raised his hand and declared, "Remember one thing—just one thing—meaning, that what I say isn't from the mentality of the low-lifers running 'round on these streets."

When he used words like 'Remember one thing', I sensed something major was coming, that he had something important to say, so I gave him my undivided attention and braced myself to receive his message as humbly as I could.

"Do you recall the Greek myth about Narcissus? You know, the one you were taught in history class?"

I nodded. "He fell into a pool and drowned while looking at his own reflection. Didn't that mean he was in love with himself or something? That's where the word *narcissistic* comes from, right?"

"Yes, and many people interpret it as conceit, but myths are made to direct attention to something a little deeper than that. That particular myth signifies the need for us to look beyond our little ego-selves. Have you ever heard the expression, *the conflict you see in others is but a reflection of what you hold within yourself?*"

"Yeah, but I can't say I understand it."

Michael shook his head while mouthing a long, "Nooo, you don't". Then he continued to explain. "Remember we just spoke about how so many people drain you, take advantage of you, and the like?"

I sighed on a long, "Yes."

"Well, did you ever stop to think that maybe you were aiming to get something from them? Maybe you were connecting to their energy because you were *sourcing* from them, instead of from within yourself?"

"What do you mean, I was *sourcing* from them? I thought Don and my roommates were taking from me?" I scoffed.

"Pay attention to what I'm saying here, dammit! They wouldn't have been able to use your energy unless you were trying to use theirs."

"What the hell are you talking about, Michael? You keep—"

"For someone with your level of intellect, you can sometimes be dumber than a box of rocks, Salvatore. Are you going to put a lid on it?" he asked testily.

"Alright, alright already." I sighed, yet again. "Go on. I'm listening."

"You looked to them, or better said, to *your idea of them* to validate your need to fix them, when it would have served everyone's best interest if they'd been awakened to their own inner resources, and then drew from them. In your wrong thinking, you placed the limitations you believed you saw in them on a pedestal, which only served as a foundation for a co-dependent relationship. One might even say you tried to do the impossible by *making limitation a God*, Salvatore. Paradoxically, they were doing the same with you! Then, in the disappointment wrought by your joint inability to fulfill each other's needs at such a level, you attracted one another's woe in a vicious cycle of resentment. But in such a clash of blind ego, none of you could possibly have lived up to the models you had set for each other. The truth of the matter is that, all of you were unconscious of real power, of your true selves. In that unconsciousness, which is the definition of limitation, you left yourselves wide open to take the brunt of such displacement. For as long as you stayed together, the energy that was trapped between your roommates, Don, and you was enough to light up New York City."

"Well—"

Michael raised a finger, cutting off my attempted explanation. "Be thankful those days have passed, because they were beginning to pull from your cell tissue. Don't cling to people under those types of circumstances. Walk away, as they are neither your source, nor you theirs. Realize there was a lesson in it for you, and nothing else. It's high time you learned it," he stated adamantly. "At unseen levels of mind, it's disempowering to people, and it can even make them angry when you act as if they can't make it without you. You also disempowered yourself when you depended on your need to make them well. Miraculously, you all managed to survive this episode, when many people in similar circumstances don't make it."

"Well, yeah, we did survive. But it took me a long time to feel like my old self again," I modestly admitted. In fact, after sharing my home and a large chunk of my life with these people, it took me more than a year to regain peace of mind. However, there was no escaping the truth that I couldn't blame it all on them. Although unconscious of the dynamics in play at the time, I was still responsible for my part in rolling out the welcome mat.

"Whatever philosophies, teachings, or acts of faith it takes to get you there, the most important lesson for you to learn from those weird situations is that you need to awaken to the fact that you've been mistaken about your own identity: *your value.* That is the root of all your pain. Instead of acting like Narcissus and succumbing to a distorted reflection of who you are in everything, be grounded in a broader perception of yourself and extend your acknowledgment of the same capability to others. It's quite freeing."

Had there been flies around, I would have caught them all as I sat gaping. I was astonished at what came forth from Michael's mouth, a man whom I'd once jokingly referred to as the *Shaman of Ipswich.*

"Regardless of what others think, there will be no need to flounder in delusion when you become grounded in your life in the here and now," he said, rising to his feet.

I followed him up and we shook the sand from our bodies, then swung our arms freely as we continued to stroll along the beach.

"As for those psychic experiences, take them as side effects of your path, and not as ends in themselves," Michael continued. "I know how it feels to have clear intuitions, and yours will become more pronounced and helpful in time. However, it's important not to take too much of a side-step by building a nest around psychic abilities, which are only an offshoot of your destiny. Stay on the middle road, and attuned to your larger purpose for which you will develop a feel."

"Okay, I won't allow for so much distraction." I'm sure the

tone of my voice mirrored the delight I found in my friend's progressively relaxed state. He radiated such warmth toward me that it placed his earlier grimness in a new light.

"Meaning you won't be hanging a *Psychic* sign on your door anytime soon?" He chuckled.

His chuckle was more like a sigh of relief that we'd had this long discussion, than amusement from his 'psychic sign' joke. I glanced out over the ocean and noticed that the waves had begun to calm with the receding tide, akin to the way Michael's mood had calmed from his recent frustration with me; for some inexplicable reason, the parallel caused anxiety to grow inside me. "I realize that we haven't known each other for very long, Michael, but you've never spoken to me with such urgency before. What's going on? Is there something else I need to know?"

Michael lowered his head, and with his hand, rubbed the back of his neck as though scanning his mind in search of the right words to say. When he turned to face me, his facial features had significantly softened, and tears had welled in his eyes. Rare are the moments, at least in my life, when someone looks at me, not with their eyes, but with their heart. The look I saw on Michael's face was one of pure compassion, and I felt it to the core of my being.

"I just want you to keep your senses intact," he said in a soothing voice. "I'm tired of watching you allow other people define and play you as a pawn in their own games of life. You have so much insight beneath the surface of your everyday mind and it often bubbles over into the words you speak. Pay attention to what you say during those times, and remember to walk your talk."

I remained silent, allowing his advice to sink into my brain as I waited for more to come.

"The thing with you, is that you have emotional loose ends that are connected to your limited sense of identity, and they always get you into a mix of trouble. The detours you take in life are evidence of this fact. These loose ends need to be tied up, Salvatore!" He exhaled deeply and loudly through his mouth, as if he'd been holding all this in for the months I'd known him, and had been waiting for the right time to let it out.

He eventually said that he was going away for a spell, and that our time together was actually to help prepare me for what he called "A journey". I had no idea what he was talking about. I hadn't known him for very long, yet it seemed like forever. If I had one word to describe the crossing of our paths, it would be *myste-rious*—mainly because there was a persistent notion that something, indefinable to me, was going on behind the scenes of our friendship.

Michael lived across the street from me, so I helped him lug his sack of petrified wood home. I was still curious and wanted to get a look at what else he'd found, but he said to wait until after he cleaned it. I had already asked him three times to show me, but apparently, he wasn't one to be pushed, so I didn't force the issue when he nonchalantly changed the subject while we said our goodbyes.

After that night, I decided it was time for some serious self-inventory. Knowing that Michael would be an anchor during my time of self-discovery, I didn't look forward to his absence. I recalled the times when I looked out my third-floor window and saw Michael standing in his yard with his arms up and his hands reaching toward the sky. His rituals in the dark appeared personal and sacred. As fascinating as it was to watch what I called his *moonlight dances*, I felt invasive to his privacy, so I never questioned him about it, nor would I ever bring it up in conversation.

I got home at 10:30 p.m., took a hot, salt bath, and crawled into bed.

The next day was a workday at the shipping and receiving department of an electrical parts fabrication company. I looked forward to seeing my funny friend and coworker, Jack, whom I affectionately referred to as Jack-in-a-box because he jumped around so much. Since I was quite vulnerable to those to whom I felt close, especially him, I was hoping he'd be funny rather than proselytizing, as he tended to be of late.

I could have sworn I heard Michael's voice echo in my head, *You can say that again!*

5

MISPLACED LOYALTIES

*"The deeper truths of life aren't limited to the words of any one philosophy,
nor are they limited to words at all. What is true is living, fluid and free—
and extends beyond the threads imparted to us, which we try to capture and
freeze into language."*

— The Author

E ven though we were both party animals in our early
twenties, Jack McLean and I stood at opposite poles of
personality. A philandering charmer, with the looks of a god, he
came on with the excitement of a Fourth of July fireworks display,
and I the flair of cardboard. He was a truckload of fun, and so
boisterous, his energy acted as an infusion of enthusiasm for me.
But alas, time would prove that we never really knew one another
at all.

With proclamations of new-found spiritual enlightenment, my
wild sidekick turned into the Pied Piper, and although he believed
that profound issues, like eternal salvation were at stake, and

worse, the horror of its alternative, I still followed him like an insipid chameleon. The people with whom he became involved told me that I was spiritually confused, and after spending months around them and their beliefs, I didn't exactly know what to believe. Then, unexpectedly, through a deductive mode of reasoning, I learned what was *not* true for me. I also discerned that they weren't the ones who would be guiding me around God Almighty's universe.

Those people called themselves Born-Again Evangelical Christians. Some of them said they were Charismatic Pentecostals. In any case, their beliefs would eventually go against the grain of my innards like sandpaper. My days of Bible study groups, and other people's scriptural interpretations came as a wake-up call while I sat among those faithful worshipers. But what exactly were they faithful to, and why?

In one breath they expounded on Bible chapters and verses that promised unconditional love, outpourings of blessings, and every spiritual gift, then in the next, they condemned those whom they deemed unworthy to be adopted by God. Understandably, they left me with a feeling of utter chagrin.

They stood boldly in their belief that even though God loved us, he would send us to hell to burn eternally; they went so far as to say that scientists had found that 'lake of fire' in outer space. Defining guilt down to a science, the group announced that we go to hell by our own choice.

If a child fell while playing in the schoolyard, they blamed Satan. They believed that the popular blue cartoon characters on Saturday morning television were evil, and were influencing their children in some way. Hundreds of contemporary record albums became fuel for a bonfire celebration because they thought there were demons in the music. They spoke of love, yet because of their stated belief that there was nothing good within them, they were incapable of loving themselves, and instead looked outward for God.

The freedom they professed turned out to be a dark road, weaving bondage to blind trust, which led to an intensified version of the fear-based religion of my childhood; thus, my disillusionment with them grew. I had questioned that religion so many years ago, yet answers were still coming, and in not-so-simple ways.

I was still looking at biblical scriptures as though through a dark glass, when out of utter desire for clarity, I touched the edge of understanding Jesus' message about a free gift. But I saw this gift differently from the way they did.

The power of persuasion can be overwhelming to a vulnerable mind, so subjecting myself to their dire warnings demanded constant reassessment of my wits to ensure that I wasn't making an irretrievable mistake which, according to them, would doom my soul to eternal damnation. Such to-and-fro soul-searching forced me to a point where I had to confront a paradox of two perspectives colliding in my head. For the sake of my sanity, I had to analyze, decipher, and reconcile every belief I had ever taken in about God.

One day, at a critical point during what I called a *shakedown*, rather than a breakdown, I sat at my kitchen table for hours delineating what was true for me and what was not. As I'd done in past years, I observed from somewhere between my thoughts, but in this case, there were two worlds of thought at hand. During the period when the devout folks in Jack's church group regarded me as weak, backslidden, and displaying no fruits of the Holy Spirit, I was at home facing every inner *demon* with the sword of truth. I confronted them over and over again, and when I finally saw them for what they were, or were not—they disintegrated. I also realized that if I were to fully understand them, the biblical terms I came across would have to be translated into their present-day meaning.

It was difficult to process the misinformation I was getting, but the time I spent doing so showed me the unnerving power of thought while simultaneously serving to strengthen my resolve. There were days when I felt abandoned, and as though I were hanging by a thread with the words, *Trust in God,* flowing through my head, while at the same time another voice shouted, *You're going to hell.*

The truth of the matter was that both voices originated from my own inner dichotomous mindset. The latter reflected the belief system I had taken in from these people. Anyone's idea that God would leave me for any reason crossed all boundaries of my intellect. I decided to trust in God. I was inwardly pulled to stop idolizing people, and so I left the group with their fear-driven use of belief, which I later came to see as part of their growth, just like it was a part of mine.

No one *allows* you to be you, and no one should be the sole interpreter of anything for you. Only you have the power to be you, and to decipher ideas and philosophies for yourself. Some people may act as supportive guides, but the bottom line is that each individual should have the freedom to process what he or she thinks about any given matter. Truth simply *is,* and it requires that we be still in order to acknowledge it.

There are people whose personalities and lifestyles seem to be complemented by the structure of their chosen ministry. I give them the respect to which they are entitled. As for me, I will never again endure the discomfort of allowing other people to walk through my head with their dirty feet. Belief can be a dangerous thing.

Associating with this congregation while holding onto my own reasoning had been a test of strength, but I wanted to be with my friend, Jack. I was following him—not them.

Despite the fact that we'd known each other long before he adopted those beliefs, disagreement over his new religious ideologies caused a rift between us that spread to all levels of our friendship. However, neither our differences, time, nor distance would break our bond, because we were, indeed, friends.

6

THE WILDERNESS

"You are not a drop in the ocean. You are the entire ocean in a drop."

— Rumi

Two weeks had passed, and I expected that Michael was back in town. I headed to the bar we frequented in hopes of finding him so we could play pool and drink lots of cold beer all night—at least I could drink, since Michael didn't.

I arrived at the bar to find the *soul-winning team* from a local church I had once visited standing outside the entrance. With strumming guitars and harmonizing chords on a portable keyboard, they burst into a heartfelt rendition of "In the Garden", one of my favorite gospel songs. After they were finished singing, I extended a friendly greeting, only to be met with silence. In fact, my very presence generated so much gloom, they were compelled to look away from me and the bar toward the other side of the street as they mumbled, "Can't face sin". Although I still had unanswered questions about God, I was glad I didn't believe in him the way they did.

China, a sweet soul whose presence graced the place, gave me a persuasive push through the door. China was a transvestite, who looked like an Asian version of Valerie Bertonelli. I never gave much thought to what was under her clothes because it really didn't matter. She was simply my friend, whose soul I came to know and accept through her eyes.

The small club was packed like a can of sardines on that Friday night, and she joked with me while carrying a shot of liqueur with a flame atop it. Laughter livened the atmosphere, and music suited to the occasion blasted on the jukebox as I made my way through the crowd toward the bar. I anticipated a cold brew hitting the spot after a long, sweaty workday. I also looked forward to seeing Michael, so needless to say, I was thrilled when he caught my eye, and motioned me to join him at his corner table. Even surrounded by other patrons, it seemed as if he was trying to keep to himself. In fact, he looked like a loner who didn't like to mingle, but that would all change, at least for tonight. After all, we had music, pool tables, and lots of beer to drink—just what the doctor ordered, so to speak.

I bought two bottles, meandered my way to Michael's table, and gave him a welcoming hug. "Hello my friend. It's great to see you!"

"You, too," he said heartily, giving me a solid pat on the back.

As I took the seat across from Michael, I noticed people gawking strangely at us. Did I have egg on my face or something? I chalked up their stares to curiosity, or perhaps envy at the joy they saw on our faces when we embraced, and gave my attention back to my friend. "So how did your trip go?" I asked cautiously, since Michael hadn't been willing to divulge much information about it before he left.

"Mission accomplished," he said, offering nothing more.

Despite the fact that mine had been an open book to him, Michael's guarded expression indicated that he was clearly being secretive about his life. I respected his privacy, but at the same time my growing frustrations and curiosity pushed me to ask, "Can you tell me where you went and what you did, at least?"

"I went to Montana to participate in a Native American ceremony."

"What kind?" I asked, both surprised and grateful that he'd given me something.

"It involved the highly, holy, sacred cleansing of the object that came into my possession the night we walked the beach."

"Really?" My eyes popped and excitement sizzled through me as I recalled that night, and Michael telling me that I must wait to see the mysterious object until after he cleaned it. I assumed he'd be washing it in his kitchen sink, not in Montana, a state clear across the continent.

Before I could erupt with an inquisition, Michael placed a reassuring hand on my shoulder, and looked directly into my eyes. "I understand your angst, but I ask that you place your trust in me and continue to be patient," he stated, most reverently. "A sublime process is unfolding, and you will receive answers to your questions soon enough. We Blackfoot know of great truths beyond words. So, just let things happen the way they will. Too many questions, too soon, will only get in the way."

I was dumbfounded for endless seconds after Michael dropped the bomb that he was a Blackfoot Native American. I became even more intrigued and puzzled as I recalled that the teachers at my spirit school had told me that my predominant Spirit Guide was a Blackfoot Chief. Could this be some kind of coincidence? Strangely, instead of being alarmed, I felt a wave of calm wash over me. I felt at peace with Michael, who always seemed to have a soothing influence on me. I trusted him with my life; that I knew for certain, even if I didn't know why.

"Here, looks like you need this," Michael said, pushing his beer in front of me. "I don't drink, as you know."

When I caught his gaze, I had the feeling that he'd deliberately interrupted my train of thoughts like he'd done that night during our last walk on the beach.

While I sat there cogitating, he let out a boisterous laugh, shot to his feet, and pulled me toward the pool table. Honoring his request not to ask more questions, I put all curiosity aside, chalked my cue stick, and decided to rock the night.

I was having a good time, in spite of the increasing number of patrons and known acquaintances from my regular visits at the bar, who kept staring and laughing at us. Some even looked sad for me, and at one point, even China sauntered near to ask how I was doing, as though something was wrong. My discomfort and confusion grew at the reactions from all these people, so I self-medicated on beer in an effort to ignore them.

As the saying went, time did fly while we were having fun—or trying to in this case—and I was undeniably inebriated by the time we left the bar. Michael proved to have the patience of a saint, presenting no protest as I repeatedly careened into him while we walked the dimly lit streets leading to our neighborhood. He dragged my drunken ass up the stairs to my apartment, then silently went on his way.

As I lay in my bed, I couldn't stop one sentence from running through my head: *Michael is a Blackfoot Indian!*

Those days were filled with great times, but admittedly, I was beginning to drink a little too much, too often, and to the point where I didn't remember some of the great times the next day. I still used alcohol and a variety of drugs like bad medicine.

Weddings, funerals, or any kind of event where people gathered required self-medication, which often resulted in my saying things I wouldn't normally say and doing things I wouldn't normally do. I even felt uncomfortable at holiday dinners with family and friends, and I sometimes ate quickly so I could escape from the dining table. I simply didn't know what was wrong with me as my Sympathetic Nervous System went awry.

Staying on an even keel became a balancing act that regularly took me one step forward and two steps back. I went to a few therapists for counsel; some of them were quite helpful, but I was too impatient to persevere through their treatments. The variety of pharmaceuticals others offered made me feel worse, so I discontinued using them within weeks. I needed answers, not something to mask my need to ask questions.

Jumping onto any available positive-thinking bandwagon helped me more than anything, even though this approach did not get to the root of my psychosomatic conundrums. Those things would be revealed to me later, but for the time being, anxiety and depression became accepted as normal parts of living. It was the discomfort of physical symptoms, such as visual disturbances and vertigo, that drove me to seek relief via illicit drugs.

My high-wire act had swung me from being out-of-work and homeless, to savoring every ounce of healing sensation a dusty pink sunset had to offer at the end of a grueling eighty-hour workweek. There were periods when everything seemed to fall into place, yet times of perplexity when I couldn't get out of my own way. I alternated between both states of mind like a passenger on a rollercoaster with a will of its own. The only consistency in my life was that there was none.

No mind likes a vacuum, so in an attempt to fill the voids he thought he witnessed in my life, my friend, *Jack-in-a-box*, told me that I had no confidence. Although I understood that there was something true to his words, they bothered me so much, I looked up the word *confidence* in the dictionary. The first definition was *trust*. How could a friend I loved think that I lacked *trust*, something I was certain we had between us?

On closer examination, I learned that the root meaning of the word stemmed from the Latin, *con*, meaning *with*, and *fidence*, meaning *fidelity*. As I dug deeper still, the meaning of Jack's statement became increasingly clear: I lacked balance in my life. What Jack perceived as my reactions to the outer world, was actually a portrayal of my discordant, internal thoughts. His statement helped me discover that I had unconsciously compartmentalized my thinking as a defense mechanism to the degree that there wasn't enough cohesiveness to form a balanced whole. It was as if my mind was comprised of parts of different puzzles thrown together into one box.

The conflicting thoughts and emotions of my inner world needed healing, but what exactly did that mean? How did this happen? I sensed it had to do with *value*—what it was and where I placed it. The study of words had always fascinated me. Etymology opened up a whole new perspective on language, leading me to a crash course in semantics and symbolism. It taught me that trust is based on consistent fidelity among thoughts, which accordingly translates to confidence within one mind, or among several minds.

On a larger scale, we've become so jaded to words that they've become habits. We often don't really hear what we say, holding only to the buzz of worn-out phrases as they bend to relate to contemporary superficiality.

Prior to self-medicating, what was there in my life that caused disharmonic thoughts? I knew there was a reason for everything, but even after a million prayers, I received no simple answers. Introspection came up against an impenetrable wall that I believed to be the edge of my mind. But remembering that at one point Michael had stressed the importance of looking within myself, I continued to do so.

I participated in numerous self-help workshops, but I always left with feelings of dissatisfaction when I failed to experience the release everyone else talked about. Some of the groups I joined were scary, and I quickly distanced myself upon deciding that their ways weren't for me. A lead person of one group stalked me for months after my departure from it. I was beginning to realize that most of the religions and various groups I had attended believed that their way of understanding was the only way, and that *they had a pathological need for agreement.*

Ocean sunsets from the west side of town were my refuge. There was something about the expansiveness of the sea that lent me pleasant contrast. Prior to one of my beach walks, I picked up Terry Cole-Whittaker's book, *What You Think of Me is None of My Business.* Her wisdom led me to immerse myself in *A Course in Miracles,* by The Foundation for Inner Peace. Absorbing the course's cyclic text demanded persistence and even courage, but the effort paid off in helping me to clear my mind.

Separating the wheat from the chaff took on new meaning when I awoke to the fact that I'd lost a sense of my own identity because I had been sourcing from other people's ideas of who I was, which was akin to what Michael had said. But then I realized that those same people had also bought into other people's ideas about who *they* should be, culminating into what I began to call, 'life's bittersweet symphony'. I don't make a religion out of anything, but as far as identity was concerned, *A Course in Miracles* was one way to help shake the cobwebs off my brain. Truth can cut into your psyche like a knife, and it can be initially painful; however, I welcomed it.

During that particular time of change, I witnessed my own questions about life as though they were being asked from another place outside of myself. But deeper observation revealed that I was actually witnessing from the place between my thoughts, which was within.

The doctor who'd diagnosed me with *anxiety and panic disorder* believed that since I had already done so much inner work, the condition might stem from repressed emotion. He suggested that I should participate in a specialized workshop, to which I agreed.

When I got there, I was told that the purpose of the process I was about to undergo was to evoke unconscious anger.

Our group of six proceeded to beat pillows with tennis rackets, engage in tugs-o-war, and partake in other activities along the same lines, while grunting, screaming, and crying. We were expected to provoke anger and then release it from our minds and bodies. Turning red was considered a good thing in this place. A pine coffin stood in a corner to remind us that we had an expiration date, and that we should strive to complete this personal endeavor. We were told to feel free to leave whenever we felt that our mission was accomplished; that sounded logical to me.

I watched as my peers became angry, some more than others. One of them cried incessantly while baring hurtful episodes of his life. I respected these brave and willing people, but when I actively participated, I was singled out and told that I wasn't 'acting up' or 'reaching into my anger' enough. When I beat the pillow wildly, still to no avail, they suggested that I should reposition myself so I could hit it even harder.

Because of a back injury that had led to surgery three years earlier, instead of kneeling, I chose to sit on my heels. I resumed beating this pillow, only to be told that my caution was a way of unconsciously guarding against releasing anger I was holding in my lower back. They also expressed their surprise that I hadn't had a heart attack because I was holding accumulated energy in my chest area.

The facilitator intermittently performed deep-tissue bodywork on my pectoral muscles and along my jawline while continuously referring to my 'awful state' and emphasizing his evaluation that I kept "hedging and hedging". I was mystified, and bruised from his deep-tissue massages.

A red flag of caution went up in me when I watched one of the participants become so angry while beating a pillow, he seemed to personify rage itself. Enough was enough. I had no desire to blindly continue with the process. If I were so out of touch with some emotion lurking within that I couldn't feel it during our sessions, maybe it didn't exist. I didn't want to feign anger, simply to blend in. Their philosophy didn't work for me at the time. I wasn't going to exacerbate my lumbar condition by following their postural suggestions. I knew my decision to leave would be regarded as the defense mechanism of denial.

Maybe I just wasn't ready, and any repressed anger would best be left alone. I had hoped the method would result in diminishing anxiety in me, but it didn't. I took the remarks about a heart attack as an unqualified opinion. I believed my barrel chest was a result of overeating and drinking too much beer, which, quite frankly, could have led to heart problems, but these people were coming from an entirely different angle. After five sessions, I was done. Leaving the building for the last time came with a sigh of relief.

While walking home, I noticed a nun standing in front of the stucco exterior of a church I often passed, and occasionally visited. Drawn by a certain peace, I entered St. Mary's to absorb its beauty and say a prayer, or just sit there in silence.

That day, the nun approached me and placed her hand on my shoulder. "My dear, you look so distraught," she said, emphatically. "Would you like to sit down and talk about anything in particular?"

As pleasant as she was, I kindly passed on her offer, and asked that she simply say a prayer for me. I was depressed, which was normal under the circumstances. I'd gotten a call the night before, informing me about yet another friend who'd died from AIDS as a result of intravenous drug use. At last count, over thirty people I knew had died from drug overdoses and AIDS in Gloucester, sometimes two or more siblings from the same family—some of them close friends and relatives who never even reached thirty years of age. I'd heard that there were hundreds more in town who were suffering from HIV infection. What the hell was going on at unseen levels with so many of the baby boomers, of not only Gloucester, but all across the nation?

I sat there thinking back to the spring of 1969 and the musical, *Hair*. There was such a beauty to the era. The vibration of the times had been felt in the air. Songs like "Good Morning Starshine", by Oliver, reminded me of my close friend, Peter. We were only fifteen years old, and drugs weren't yet a part of our lives. Peter was beautiful. He was a happy kid with an infectious laugh, and eyes that sparkled. That all changed over the years, and now he was gone.

My friend, Anne, was always looking for a laugh. She was witty and knew how to catch us off guard with her dry sense of humor. Then, there was Donnie. I remember hearing my friends say that Donnie had more soul in his little finger, than Jiffy had peanut butter. There were the many young girls I'd watched grow up, and who I never imagined would come to this end. But they did. All of these people were beautiful souls who were gone, far too soon. My friends were dying, and it was a common occurrence. Sadness overwhelmed me. Not the crying kind, but a deep ache. Not just for my loss, but for all who lost—maybe because I remembered the good times.

These weren't issues I wanted to discuss with the kind nun. I really didn't want to talk with anyone about anything. The disarray of the past week sought only solitude and the peace of sunbeams shining through stained-glass windows.

QUOTE

"Be generous towards those who are in need or less favored than you. Arrange things every day so that you do at least one good deed for someone else. Whatever your good deed, do not boast, but thank God for enabling you to contribute to the well-being of others."

— From The Rosicrucian Code of Life #9

7

THE FORETELLING

"One cannot help but be in awe when one contemplates the mysteries of eternity, of life, of the marvelous structure of reality."

— Albert Einstein

I sat quietly that night in the blue casting of a full moon, gazing vacantly at the reflection of plants bouncing off the glass tabletop in my kitchen. The time I spent with the nun at St. Mary's reminded me of an experience I had, years before, with another nun from St. Agatha's parochial school that was adjoined to the church of my youth.

One morning in 1962, with that nun in hot pursuit, I bolted from the sidewalk and into the street only to freeze up at the sound of screeching rubber. My palms stung as they landed on the hood of a Chevrolet, and as my eyes collided with the petrified face of the woman behind the wheel, a claw-like hand emerged from the black and white cloth that had been chasing me, and snatched me by the scruff of my shirt.

"Where were you at nine o'clock mass on Sunday?" Sister Clementus screamed, as she mercilessly shook me.

"I was there, Sister," I replied, still stunned from my first near-death experience.

"You could have given that woman a heart attack."

What the heck! I thought. *St. Agatha's isn't even my school and I have to put up with this?*

She used to chase me regularly as I made my way to the public school I attended, just two blocks away. Her talk about the devil, sin, and hell, assured me of my due punishment for dreaded blasphemy—the only unpardonable sin—whatever that meant. As I laid in bed each night, the word "BLASPHEMY" would flash in my mind as I envisioned hellish lakes of fire. That disturbing experience was one of many that would later lay the groundwork for my explorations and questions about religion and self.

In comparing the two nuns, I concluded that the one at St. Mary's had a warm, kind heart, while Sister Clementus' was stone cold. There was no doubt in my mind that my experiences with the latter was the reason I preferred to be alone in churches. I went to sleep with the comfort of knowing that the nun from St. Mary's was praying for me.

I always questioned life, so it was no wonder that by the time I reached the age of twenty-two, my quest led me to the teachings of Universal Law by the Masters of an ancient mystery school, of which I later became an initiate. I was introduced to metaphysics as a pathway leading to *Christ Consciousness,* as they called it.

Just as with Michael's, through their instruction I realized that I still viewed almost everything through the beliefs and opinions of others, a habit that creates a displaced sense of self. The teachings explained the dynamics of belief, and that what *is* believed is actively reflected as the believer's reality, from the screen of life. For example: if I change my attitude about any given situation, my perception responds like the turn of a kaleidoscope, and creates a new reality.

They taught that human beings are *electromagnetic* or *spiritual* in nature and, possess minds that have the ability to either *project* superficial thinking or *extend* from a deeper truth.

The day after Michael told me that he was a Blackfoot Indian, I retrieved past lessons I'd received from the mystery school. To avoid the possibility of confabulation on my part, I wanted to know exactly what they had to say about my connection to the Blackfoot. This is what I read: "You are privileged to have a powerful spirit guide, one who radiates every color of the rainbow, which is symbolic of great wisdom. In a recent incarnation, he was a Blackfoot Chief, whose tribe roamed the plains." So, there it was in black-and-white, for whatever it was worth.

I wondered why this guide had chosen me, and despite my intrigue, apprehension grew just before the arrival of each successive lesson. I would eventually discover how this uneasiness was directly related to long-forgotten events in my past that were being slowly uprooted through the lessons and, in every other way I had been learning. I wasn't aware of it then, but time would show that the truth, so often left uncultivated, is a foundational truth that is closely linked to *core-identity*.

I arrived home from work early one day and joked with the postman as he placed the familiar envelope from the mystery school into my mailbox. I stood there thinking about the lessons for a moment. I knew they were transformative, but why were they lifelong? I believed transforming one's life was what the teachers meant by metamorphosis, but the notion that the terms had different meanings began to rise in my mind.

The more I learned about processing and eliminating negative belief patterns, the more I felt that the walls around my thinking were crumbling and restructuring into new perspectives, or into the horizon of a 'beyond' that I couldn't yet see. My intertwined mental, emotional, and physical states oscillated between a sense of freedom and feelings of dread, brought on by letting go of the familiar and looking toward the unknown. I sometimes wanted to go back to my old self and pull the covers over my head, which was another paradox, since through the process of the teachings, much of that self with which I had identified, was gone.

I inhaled, then exhaled through pursed lips while pondering over just how much of a change I was looking at here. I whisked the envelope from my mailbox and climbed the stairs of the Victorian I called home, all the way up to the third-floor hallway that led to my room.

After tossing the unusually thick envelope onto my desk, I glanced at it curiously for a few minutes before I sat down and opened it. Supplemental to my biweekly lesson, there was a sealed, blue scroll encircled by a golden ribbon. Information in an attached fold described its contents as a *Foretelling,* and stated that I had the option whether or not to read the *"Solemn truth"* inside.

The foretelling of a solemn truth? What could they possibly mean by that? These kinds of situations upset me. A knot formed in my stomach, and I wished they hadn't sent it to me. Despite my discomfort, curiosity got the best of me, and like Pandora with her box, I removed the ribbon and broke the seal. To help calm my nerves, I poured some water from my carafe and took a few sips before I unrolled the fine paper of the scroll. It read:

You are about to embark on an inter-dimensional journey where you will reconcile that which has caused you great tribulation. When faced with opposition, remember to focus on the seed of truth growing within you; for when you know truth, you will see there is nothing to fear.

The implications of that statement crossed the limits of my sensibility. Was this the same journey Michael had mentioned? How could that be? He never said that he was an initiate of the mystery school. Certainly, he'd said that our talks were to help prepare me for a journey. I took that to mean we were going on a trip, somewhere. Maybe to some far-out place like Bhutan in the Himalayas or, the Great Pyramid of Egypt. But what did an *interdimensional journey* mean? The knot in my stomach turned to nausea. Where was I going?

Not only was I about to find out, but I would also later realize that I had to go *there* in order to live more fully *here*.

8
_____

AN ALTERNATE REALITY

"Many teachers will tell you to believe; then they put out your eyes of reason and instruct you to follow only their logic. But I want you to keep your eyes of reason open; in addition, I will open in you another eye, the eye of wisdom."

— Sri Yukteswar

I've often heard that it's best to live each day to the fullest. On the following day, I discovered the reason for that advice. After the fact, my buddy, Jack, told me that I was knocked unconscious when a storage bin collapsed on top of my head. I recalled nothing of this accident. My only recollection was of our morning break, a flood of colors, and then finding myself in a church full of people, with whom I seemed very well acquainted.

I felt disoriented in this church in which I was obviously having an 'otherworldly' experience. There was no reason for me to think that I had been knocked unconscious in some other life, because I didn't remember any other. All I knew was that I was in the church, sitting next to a man named Ray.

"Feeling okay, brother?" Ray asked.

"I'm fine, thanks, just a little dizzy from the heat, I guess," I replied, woozily.

I watched as Suzanne, an elder of the Gospel Lighthouse Church, and who was dressed in a gray ankle-length dress, strode purposefully to her place adjacent to the pulpit, as though assigning herself guardian of all things sacred. I listened intently as the pastor rose to speak, but nothing he said reached inside me to revitalize my life. I needed relativity, something to ring true on Sundays, but all I got were contradictions and proclamations pointing to the possibility of eternal separation from God.

As parishioners whispered, "Blasphemer!" and, "Plucked right from the flock!" I wondered if I had a reprobate mind, the term used to describe the spiritually incorrigible. They evidently thought that I lacked faith because I was known to ask too many questions.

One time, Suzanne told me that the Holy Spirit would shut the door of reformation in my face for becoming amused when during a service, a woman spun her head wildly, her hair whipping around in a two-foot radius, as she spoke in tongues. I was rejected and denied the promise of the unconditional love I'd so often heard about, but never felt from these haughty-eyed people, especially not from the women with the beehive hairdos.

During this Sunday service, an acquaintance by the name of Sandy sat across the aisle from me. She appeared shaken, as though she'd just drank a pot of strong coffee. From my own experiences with the disorder, I recognized her behavior as an oncoming anxiety and panic attack, which could be extremely frustrating, especially in public. I thought that perhaps we could develop a supportive relationship since we suffered from the same ailment. Having someone to talk with might help to lighten her burden, but since I always tried to hide my own symptoms from others, I knew that I would have to approach the subject with Sandy in a diplomatic way, and at another time.

I expected the compassion I felt for Sandy to bear fruit in some way, but through a turn of events, I discovered the universe sets a time and place for everything. I wouldn't be talking with Sandy anytime soon. Further into the sermon, I went to the rest room, and upon returning, I looked over to where Sandy was sitting, but she was gone. When I asked of her whereabouts, one of the male members pointed to the window facing the parking lot, and laughingly said, "Sandy flipped out."

I looked out the window to see Sandy talking with Suzanne while they both stood in the parking lot. Sandy was crying. I felt compelled to go out and rescue her when a van pulled up, and two men, both of whom I later discovered were Sandy's brothers, hopped out. They struggled to get her into the van while Suzanne tried her best to hold her back. After they drove away, Suzanne came back inside, brittle and stone-faced as ever, and sat in her place near the podium. The events of the past ten minutes were yet to come to light, but there was nothing I could do for Sandy now. She was gone.

I turned to watch an elderly, black woman, who was visiting from the south, walk to the front of the church. Adorned in a pristine yellow gown, her elegance lit up the platform as she prepared to sing. Her face radiated such warmth that I wanted to stay, but Suzanne's continuous disapproving scowl made me feel uneasy, like an unwanted guest. Her covert assaults on my psyche were so unbearable, I stood to my feet and headed down the aisle, feeling defeated, for the last time. My footsteps reverberated to dissociating stares as I left the church, but I didn't care.

Making my way to a quiet patch of grass among the tall pines across the street, I sat to the angelic tones of "Amazing Grace" echoing from the walls of the church, as the lovely, old woman sang. I reached into my pocket for the picture of Jesus my mother had given me, and was taken aback when it grew noticeably warm in my hand. While gazing at the picture and seeking forgiveness for wrongs I didn't even know I'd committed, I held to what faith remained in the promise of asking.

In that moment, a strange tingling sensation ran through my body as I was simultaneously engulfed by a scent, akin to lilac. To my surprise, a woman appeared out of nowhere and sat next to me. She placed her hands on my shoulders, turned me to face her, and held my hands. She was dressed in white silk that draped down from her head, and her skin was startlingly translucent. She looked vaguely familiar, and I felt comforted by her soft smile. Through eyes that seemed to embody the breadth of oceans, her gaze penetrated to the depths of me. I sat entranced in this most beautiful fragrance, and as my body elevated slightly off the ground, the thought, 'Life is about being', rose in my mind.

A softness that seemed to inhabit every color of the rainbow surrounded us when she pressed something solid against my palm. As I floated in the aura of her kindness, I saw, what I could only describe as, *Holy Symbols of Truth,* shining more silver, than silver, itself, moving across upper space in front of me. What these symbols conveyed to me dispelled all illusions of separation from God. A final display in verse read:

> *Forgiveness is the recognition of what is inherent in your being from the beginning of time. You can never lack what is "given" at the "fore" of Creation. You only need to remember and to extend this truth to others, even if necessarily from a distance.*

In that timeless moment, I knew *the peace that passeth understanding,* and the unity of everything. Then I heard a voice calling urgently to me from a distance, becoming louder and louder...

"Sal, are you all right under there? Wake up, Sal!"

"Who are you?" I asked, as a hum faded from my ears, and

tingling warmth radiated from the palm of my left hand to the crown of my head. After a few moments, it dawned on me that I was laying on the concrete floor at my workplace, where my accident had occurred, I would later learn.

"What do you mean, "Who are you?", Salvatore? It's Jack! Are you alright under there?"

A fallen storage bin lay suspended on a broken concrete slab, just inches above my body, keeping me out of full view of my coworkers. "I'm okay," I answered, still unaware of exactly what had happened. All I knew was that I was trapped.

There was increasing heat in my left hand, that was wedged between my hip and the collapsed bin. Was my hand injured? I contorted my head and neck in an attempt to inspect what I thought to be a hand wound, and saw, instead, an object glistening in an array of colors. My heart raced. What was this? My hand was now hot. Was I somehow on fire? Panic began to set in.

With unnerving anticipation, I jostled around in this cramped space, and dragged my hand up the side of my body toward my face for a closer look. I knew what I saw in my hand was some kind of crystal. But what unfolded as I gazed into this unearthly *crystalline gemstone,* both fascinated and baffled me.

I'd heard that colors have an effect on people, but these colors were permeated with a certain lusciousness, activating sensations, new to me. I was swimming in a living rainbow, until the creaking of the metallic storage bin I lay under distracted me. Heavy footsteps scurried near, and despite the danger looming above, my thoughts gravitated toward my magnificent find that cooled as I tucked it into my pocket.

Two paramedics snaked their way under the bin and slid me out of danger. Following a quick examination, they fastened me to a flat-board and carried me to an awaiting ambulance. I was rushed to the local hospital emergency room and admitted for twenty-four hours of observation.

Bewilderment and joy were what I would have considered strange bedfellows, but those were the emotional tones blanketing me as I lay in my hospital bed. Images of people in a church flooded my mind, leaving me confused as to why I was there. More confounding was the feeling that I knew them. I was just talking with someone there, but I couldn't remember whom. I must have been there, in that place, or why else would it feel so real—like life before and after my accident?

Even if there was truth to the idea of bilocation, I still couldn't wrap my mind around how I could be in two places at once. Could a ding to the head be medical grounds for strange ideations of another reality? Wherever I'd been, I knew the people, and I hadn't thought of *here*, while I was *there*. Some say the answers we seek are in our questions, but so far, I'd gotten none.

Exhaustion rolled over me like an opiate fog bank, but before I reached the shores of slumber, I felt the incessant nagging of some unfinished task. *Sandy!* Wait a minute. Who was San…

An unusually long sleep that continued into the next day came to an end when a nurse woke me to take my blood pressure. Afterwards, as lay on the hospital bed, I came to understand why 'dream study' experts stressed the importance of logging your dreams immediately upon waking. But on this occasion, it was events of the previous day that were becoming foggy, at best.

I struggled to piece fragments of memory together in some type of order. Thoughts of a church associated with a sense of displacement, a picture of Jesus, and images of a loving mother figure, along with an incredible sense of exaltation, were passing away quickly—like strands in the wind. Excitement arose in my chest, as if I were awaiting the final scene of a melodramatic opera. But the fleeting pictures on my mental screen faded to black, and with a final receding wave, I forgot everything.

Despite my failed efforts to remember the events, the afterglow in which I basked left a sense of something, too real to be misconstrued as a dream or an injury-induced hallucination. Whatever the case, my absence of memory digressed to the dismal feeling of losing the love of my life at sixteen. The first love that slipped so easily right through the palm of my…

"THE GEMSTONE!" The nurse, who was still in the room, jumped when I bellowed. "Nurse! Where are my clothes? Bring me my pants!"

Oh, God, I thought. Could this be real? How could I have forgotten the strange object that was in my hand while I lay under the collapsed bin, the day before? I was shaking.

"Your clothes are right there in the closet, Mr. DiSanti," the discombobulated nurse murmured. "I'll get them for you."

She was walking toward the closet when a loud crash outside my room caused her to change course. I couldn't contain myself, so in my barely dressed state, I rose from the bed and raced to the closet behind the door. I probed inside my pants pocket, and my spirits sank when my fingers connected with the hole loose change had poured through, twice, the previous day. With a racing heart, I fumbled around for the other pocket and sighed inwardly when my knuckles bumped against something hard. As I slid my hand inside, I felt the smooth solidity of tangibility, at last.

My breathing slowed as I retrieved my trembling hand from this pocket of serendipity. The crystal rested in my palm—proof that what we think to be dreams may very well be realities. This profundity was about to grow more apparent in the mind-boggling succession of events that would come to be known as my *inter-dimensional journey*.

9

LIFTING THE VEIL

"Believe nothing, no matter where you read it, or who said it, no matter if I have said it, unless it agrees with your own reason and your own common sense."

— Buddha

While sitting on the edge of the hospital bed, I felt the crystalline object grow warm in my hand again. My memory returned to some extent when a play of communication presented itself in the same upper-frontal space that I simultaneously associated to my previous day's experience with the translucent woman.

I put my pen to work in a vigorous attempt to capture and translate a geometrical language, which was streaming like ticker-tape across the area in front of my forehead. But writing was as inefficient a media to fully translate this information, as a toothbrush in painting a masterpiece. What seeped into my understanding of this odd, yet vaguely familiar conveyance, had a lot to do with maligned human perception. Due to conditioned repetitive thinking, there is something amiss in our ability to use inner mechanisms that generate perspective. As a result, everything we see is incorrect, and out of context with universality.

The numerical properties of the geometry embodied specific meaning that came across with the quickness of electricity. I understood the meaning to a degree, but I lost focus at the slightest distraction.

Even though I was removed at intervals from this ultra-communicative experience, I still sensed its telling. This mathematical language established that, contrary to the general thinking of the world, there is no separation in multiplicity. Humanity tends to believe that everything is divided into totally separate forms, including people and mindsets, but this isn't the case. In fact, this flawed belief is the root cause of the perpetual conflict that leads to misery on this planet.

Further clarification denoted that there's nothing wrong with multiplicity in the world, since it's the natural manifestation of variety in life. However, we must remember that all things come from singularity and that everything is extended from a unified field; therefore, we *are* a unified field.

The transmission of information wasn't only on a mental level; it also interfaced with my physicality. I felt as though every integral moving part inside me was being overhauled and lubricated, leaving me with an inner sensation of optimal synchronicity.

As I continued to absorb the information, I began to understand that we've lost sight of our true identity because we have forgotten this natural principle of unity. Something is missing, but we just don't know it. In other words, because we're unconsciously based in incompleteness, the world appears as incomplete, and as if it consists of independent, isolated forms. Everything is permeated with an *illusion of lack*, resulting in an idiopathic feeling of neediness. From our level of evolution, this circumstance was described as intrinsic to human perception, and that the pain it causes spurs us to become introspective. Fortunately, the suffering woven into the psychology that underlies our experience of the world can be used to our benefit in its call to be understood.

As my mind became increasingly permeated with information, I interpreted it to mean that in an effort to serve our ongoing evolution, we must acknowledge our overall perception as a another 'sense' tool of the mind, just as we acknowledge the sensory organs in our bodies. The level of understanding this kinetic message was in exact ratio to one's understanding of his or her universal identity, which is the governing factor that determines perspective. This holy transmittal implied that the world was leaving a dense, third-dimensional holding pattern, where its people have been defining themselves by the temporal tool of perception and fear, rather than through knowledge of the soul, which is beyond perception and eternal. This was profound. To me, it meant that the human race is in the throes of ascending in consciousness to the fourth, and then fifth dimensions, and beyond!

It wasn't that the information coming through was negative in any way. It's just that I wasn't used to being force-fed, and that's what seemed to be happening here. I was being filled to capacity, and it was becoming uncomfortable. I sat on the bed, trembling like the heat-stricken little bird I once held in the palm of my hand.

My mind raced to keep up with the set velocity of these cascading thoughts. They wouldn't stop, and to add to my distress, I realized that I couldn't move. It was as though electricity had seized my musculature in a tetanic contracture. I knew better than to resist, so I reluctantly went along with it.

Then another new perspective was imparted to me: I saw life and the material world as aspects of something greater than what I could have ever known; this greatness was expressed through a multitude of electromagnetic polarities, right down to the elemental dust of the earth. This perspective presented no specific point where the properties of a particular category of manifestation, such as temperature, changed to its opposites of hot and cold, for example. In the same way, it did not show any distinct line of separation between the colors of the spectrum.

Everything in Creation was seen as a frequency of vibration, and as aspects of *The Primordial Vibration,* also described as *The Universal Intelligence,* and THE WORD, as written in the biblical John 1:1.

The event of Creation was compared to The Big Bang when the *mental substance* of The Universal Intelligence dispersed outwardly from a point of singularity until it fragmented into levels of blind individuality. In this baptism of our divinity beneath the waters of denser consciousness, singularity was then forgotten in what is otherwise known as *involution* or—*The Fall,* as personified by Adam and Eve in the garden. We are now resurrecting in *evolution*, returning to whence we came. The frequency of human consciousness will continue to increase, propelling us to higher octaves of living as we rise slowly out of the murky water to the Self-Actualization of Christ Consciousness.

In my heightened vision, I saw that this dispersed mental substance, which is the universe, was pliable according to our thinking. I understood this to mean that our mentality has an effect on everything, and that we have the ability to consciously direct it to affect change.

As the information continued to pour forth, my mind's eye saw unconscious habitual thinking, juxtaposed with voluntary conscious thinking to create with mentality; the former showed what it means to be at *effect* of mentality, and the latter opened the way to being *cause* of one's reality.

My body relaxed. I could move again, and at this point I could have chosen to abruptly end my hook-up with this energetic transference, but as the velocity of the energy began to subside, I decided to stay and allow for a gradual release.

As I thought about the illusory perception of the material world as being solid and set, my mind gravitated to the people I knew who believed that since everything here is an illusion, nothing mattered. However, through this difficult, yet blessed, energetic opening of my eyes, I surmised that what is considered illusory from a higher perspective isn't illusion to those of us who live on the material level. Although our experiences are temporal and shall pass, we still sense them as real; therefore, they matter. We are universal beings with faculties attuned to the frequencies of the physical dimension, which leaves us subject to its inherent physical laws. But then, this stream of information hinted at *higher laws* that when used correctly, could alter our current understanding of physical laws. However, I wasn't yet able to grasp them fully.

While sitting on the bed, I felt an All-Powerful completeness draw near, one that my multiplicious mind could not withstand. After all, I was a highly conditioned human who still identified with my organic senses, mostly. I was accustomed to appraising things sequentially as external separate pieces in order to formulate a point of view I hoped would enable me to find and adapt to my place in the world. How could I hold on to the glimpse I'd caught through this unusual perspective, long enough to garner a fuller appreciation of its meaning, particularly where these higher laws were concerned?

Despite my lack of comprehension, I began to contemplate becoming a cause of my reality rather than remaining reactive to thousands of years of collective conditioning. I reveled in the prospect of becoming a conscious-mental-unit manifesting with a renewed mind in the plasticity of the mental universe. The dread I once felt for the unknown was being reinterpreted as my unfamiliarity with power, and beginning to thaw into excitement, as well.

I was interrupted when Jack arrived to drive me home from the hospital. Apparently, I'd been given a clean bill of health. He was quiet, almost morose, and he looked at me one too many times with expectancy.

"Hey, Sal. How are you feeling, turkey head?" he asked. "I thought you were dead under that collapse," he added in an unsuccessful attempt at humor.

"Boy, am I glad to see you, Jack," I said, with a slight quiver in my voice. I lied. Jack's appearance had caught me off guard. Left off kilter by my unnerving interlude with the geometric language, it was hard for me to mask my emotions on cue.

I hid the crystalline treasure from his sight before slipping it back into my pocket. I could tell he sensed something was up, but there was no way I would divulge anything pertaining to my recent experiences, especially while still trying to figure them out for myself.

Jack was obviously shaken from seeing the bin fall on top of me. The nurse had told me earlier that he'd sat quietly in my room for much of the night, and had occasionally dabbed my face with a damp cloth while I slept. She added that at one point she'd been glad to hear our voices, which could only mean that I was talking in my sleep.

Anxious to say goodbye to the hospital bed and my bemused nurse did make Jack a welcome sight. But, why was he so mum in the car with his look of expectancy bordering on restraint? As we drove away from the parking lot, I wondered if Jack's strange behavior was a result of something I'd said while talking in my sleep.

Sometimes people are connected in mysterious ways, which was the case with Jack and me. On a trip we took to Lake Tahoe, two years earlier, we explored the territory on his motorcycle. While pulling into a town called Incline Village, I could have sworn we'd entered some kind of time warp at the start of a string of uncanny events. Every time I spoke, Jack told me he was, "Just about to say that." It was the same for me whenever he spoke, not just once or twice, but disconcertingly so every time we opened our mouths to speak before we got off the bike, and also for the thirty minutes we sat on the trunk of a fallen sequoia. Jack had looked perplexed and had let out a long "Dang!" as we shook our heads in disbelief.

Recalling that trip, I remembered when we left the main road to drive down a trail leading to a state park in the rural village. The panorama that opened to us was stunning. Sloping toward the left side of the lake for quite a distance, the view of the incline captured me with the surreal quality of a silent movie. Clusters of people scattered throughout the sprawling landscape were strangely familiar to me, as were scant passersby.

Despite the eeriness of this apparent vortex, I'd floated in a sea of emotion. I felt connected to everything around me when all of it coalesced into a sudden, overwhelming nostalgia. I became buoyant with love for the place and everyone in sight. Jack and I wordlessly glanced at each other as the certainty that we'd been there before set in. The enchantment of the place was so palpable, it left me breathless. I had a feeling that we once lived entwined with that environment, and that something ancient and profound had occurred there, something that was connected with Jack and me, but which remained a mystery for the time being.

Quietly blown away, we got back onto his motorcycle and left Incline Village to be distracted, once again, by the concerns of everyday life. Jack never elaborated on that slice of time, except to chalk it up to déjà vu. "Things like that happen sometimes," he'd said, nonchalantly. But curiosity always got the best of me, and the memory of the events of that day had evoked enough questions to last a lifetime.

Jack had no trouble expressing his affectionate side during the early months of our friendship. I got more loving hugs from him in one week than I had gotten in my whole life. His arm had become like a fixture wrapped around my neck. I looked forward to his affection because somewhere along the line, for whatever reason, I grew to be infatuated with him. This felt beautiful and awkward at the same time, because Jack was straight as a board, and I was so infrequently affected in this way by the same sex, that I would not categorize myself as gay. Strangely enough, the few times I reciprocated his ongoing displays of fondness for me, it became evident that he was homophobic. The irony was that although I had a large capacity to feel, I didn't need or want anything sexual to happen between us. I wouldn't have cared if he had no genitals at all. I just knew that through our relationship, I'd discovered how possible it was for me to love a man.

Jack drove toward my place with hardly a word spoken between us. Was he largely disassociating from me like many involved with religious sects often do with those whom they believe had gone astray? I didn't think so, especially after the nurse had said he'd stayed with me for hours the night before.

Although I knew his beliefs gave rise to the concerns he had about my soul, the situation only strengthened my desire to understand why Jack never considered looking at things in other ways. Once, when he made dire pronouncements about my stance with God, I responded with a quote from Jack Kerouac, the beat poet of the 1950s: "Walking on water wasn't built in a day". It had generated a delightful half-smile from the old pal I once knew.

THE FIRST STAIRWELL LANDING

"The best and most beautiful things in the world cannot be seen or even touched. They must be felt with the heart."

— Helen Keller

Jack deposited me at the curb, and I walked the path leading from the sidewalk to the front entrance of my home. I sat on the porch steps, perplexed by the flow of information I'd received in the hospital, and the manner in which it had come.

I removed my shirt and leaned back against the third step for support while my chest drank up the heat of the sun. I moved my head slowly from side to side, and then forward and back to release the muscles in my neck.

I took a deep, cleansing breath, thinking, that by relaxing, I could get back to the mental state I was in before Jack had arrived to drive me home from the hospital. I wanted to remember all of what I knew lay just beneath the surface of my current thoughts.

I turned my head to the left again. Although somewhat blinded by the mid-morning sun, my mailbox appeared in my line of vision. A rush of adrenaline ran through me when I recalled the reference to an inter-dimensional journey in my last mystical lesson.

Sitting upright, I retrieved the newfound crystalline gemstone from my right front pocket and set it gently on my palm. As the sun shone on this mesmerizing gem, glittering with the seven colors of the rainbow, I asked myself if I'd ever seen anything so beautiful. The answer was no. At intervals, its transparent interior gave birth to gradients of light, resembling an aluminum Christmas tree, sparkling with the brilliance projected through a turning color-wheel.

Holding my oval find closely to my eyes, like I had done under the collapsed storage bin, I marveled at the hues encircling me. The same luscious sensations I had felt while trapped under the bin rose from within, transporting me to what felt like a threshold that led into the realm of colors.

I heard a distant hum, and then the colors whirled and parted like mist, opening to a great expanse. I became so overwhelmed at being drawn into this heretofore unknown vastness that I hastily turned away with a gasp.

Even knowing that the object had a significant association with the recent events I struggled to piece together, its existence was still a mystery. I sat staring into space, unable to rationalize what had just happened. I intoned one long *OM* to help regain equilibrium, and my wind chimes acquiesced to a wistful breeze that perfected the moment.

Feeling a stiffness in my back, I rose slowly and turned to step across the threshold to the front entrance of my home. The beauty in my hand grew warmer still as I made my way up the stairs. My gaze briefly shifted to the clock on the wall as I neared the top. It was 10:08 a.m.

I stepped onto the first stairwell landing, only to stop dead in my tracks when my scalp grew taut, and the hair on my head and arms stood at attention. Some magnetic force backed me against the wall, and I became instantly entranced by three apparitions, standing less than six feet in front of me. The one in the middle was tall and wore the headdress of an Indian Chief. I recognized him with the awakening of a sleeping, early childhood memory. He was the Indian I used to see in the window at the bottom of the stairs in the hallway of my old house. The intermingling rays of light emanating from the other two beings seemed to act as stabilizers for the frequency of vibration during this interfacing.

Since I was cognizant enough to know that I couldn't see them with my physical eyes, I knew I was seeing them in a somewhat preternatural way. All three beings felt electrical, and they collectively emitted a charge that activated a distinct ability in me to perceive them through new and unfamiliar senses. My whole body tingled from the experience. As though someone had flipped a switch, my progressive awareness of the beings came in tandem with the awakening memories of events from the previous day. These memories included details about the church and the translucent woman, as well as others from my distant past.

In the same way I had experienced the Holy Symbols during my encounter with the translucent woman outside the Gospel Lighthouse Church, and also with the geometrical language that had appeared to me on a screen through an aperture while I was in the hospital, I stepped into a sensational, audio-visual *movie* of myself as a young boy. It was 1962, and I was fleeing across a street into the path of an oncoming vehicle.

Tires screeched as the driver hit the brakes, and my hands landed on the hood of the car. Terror-stricken, I turned in surrender to face the wrath of the frightening nun rushing toward me. But in a welcome surprise, the hands reaching out from the folds of the religious garb were not the cold claws of Sister Clementus of yesteryear, but a kinder version of her in this re-run of the event. As she embraced me in front of the car that almost hit me, her expressions of high compassion permeated into every cell in my body.

The nun had left this earth over ten years ago. *Why am I seeing her now in this vision?* I asked myself. She'd abused me terribly in the past, yet forgiveness was automatic as I recalled the conveyances of both the geometric language and the Holy Symbols. All grievances became like chaff taken away by the wind, but I was still confused and shaken by the strength of her presence.

My anxiety increased as the incongruity of this experience, along with everything else that had happened in the last two days hit me like an emotional undertow. I felt a sudden energetic shift in the atmosphere. Although I didn't actually hear a voice, I got the distinct impression that I was being addressed by the tall chief in front of me. His attention to me proved effective when the fight-or-flight impulse from seconds ago unraveled into serenity. I felt as if my body consisted of fabric that just had all its wrinkles removed by some fabulous infusion. *Who needs drugs?* I thought, as I exhaled on a deep sigh.

In the continuity of this living vision taking place on the first stairwell landing of my home, I found myself outside the Gospel Lighthouse Church, sitting on the grass with the translucent woman. The endlessness in her eyes enveloped me, and to my amazement, she told me she was Sister Clementus. As part of her reparation to me for the occurrences of 1962, she said that she was here to assist with my evolution. Strangely enough, she looked about thirty years of age, yet, I remembered reading long ago that Sister Clementus died at age eighty-three.

In an apparent answer to my thoughts about her youthfulness, she surprised me when she said, "You are correct. I no longer live in the world of form as you do, but I do still live. Some time after I knew you as a child, erroneous belief systems were cleared from my mind. This allowed the Vital Life Force to flow unimpeded within me. My appearance changed then, but I've transformed even more since I left your dimension. I have become more conscious of what I am as a being of light that's emanated by a Greater Light," she added graciously.

I was astounded and momentarily speechless.

"You've conceptualized universal truth through your studies, and actually experienced it through the Holy Symbols. Have you not, Salvatore?"

"Yes— I have, Sister," I replied tentatively, "but in an inconsistent sort of way. I'm unable to retain all that was imparted to me by both the holy symbols and the geometric language. There were intermittent degrees of clarity during and after the experiences, but now it has escaped me."

The sister's expression indicated that she understood why I had such a lapse, so I listened as she shared her wisdom.

"As an electromagnetic being, your thoughts are a rhythmic frequency of vibration. In fact, everything has a rhythm to it, including the evolution of consciousness where a process involving your understanding of higher knowledge occurs in your concept of time. This rhythm is synchronistic with the changing frequency of your overall thinking. Your inconsistent ability to hold on to this new knowledge is a result of the expansion and contraction of consciousness, due to your prior conditioning."

Her explanation of my forgetfulness didn't open the halls of wisdom to me, but it certainly raised my curiosity.

"All energy seeks balance. In accordance with Harmonic Law, variances in frequencies of vibration will waver as they draw close to a balance within their respective octave. This law also applies to your individual system of thought. I'll take it a step further and say, *You are thought,* at a deeper level, Salvatore, and through your study and contemplation of the natural laws of the universe, you are raising the vibration of your surface mind to that of your inner being."

"I am *thought*, Sister?"

"Yes!" she said promptly.

The sister's statement was in line with the message that the geometric language had tried to convey to me. I still didn't completely understand it, so I was glad when she explained it further.

"As an extension of the Universal Intelligence, you are a *Thought of God*. The thoughts of your superficial mind are encompassed by the larger thought you are—you are, meaning the place where you truly live, and move, and have your being. The goal is for you to ultimately identify with the thought, *you are*, rather than with your conditioned surface thinking."

"I'm not trying to be funny, but in order for it to make sense, I'm going to have to think hard about what you just said."

"You already think too much. You need to learn to still your busy mind."

"Isn't that what I'm learning through the teachings of the mystics, though?"

"Yes, it is. However, stilling your mind would help you to understand how your current learning conflicts with the way you were previously trained to think. Your old way of thinking is an energetic habit that pulls on you, and as a result this conflict creates an electromagnetic polarization of your two systems of thought. When your thinking fluctuates, you become non-receptive to the positive pole of higher knowledge, and you revert to duplicating onto the screen of life from your negative pole of lesser awareness."

"I've often heard that what we don't know can't hurt us, so is it really all that bad to be less aware?"

"Take another look at the world, and then rethink your question," she said. "Humanity suffers because of ignorance, but these terms aren't used here to denote ideas of good and bad. They are about perspective, and they pertain to the mental integration that all learning requires."

"So, my thoughts are integrating with a new way of thinking, but my old way of thinking resists the process?" I asked, while repositioning my body to alleviate the discomfort in my left foot that had fallen asleep.

"Yes, but resistance is a natural part of the process, so don't resist the resistance. Not only are you integrating new thought, but through such new thought frequencies, you are also activating parts of your body that have been dormant," the sister added.

"Activating parts of my body?" I asked, wondering if in her last statement, she had associated my attempts to move into a more comfortable position with my 'mental resistance'.

"Oh! Yes," she exclaimed.

"What does my body have to do with anything?" I asked with a dubious frown.

"Your body is intertwined with your mind in ways you are yet to understand. You aren't separate from your body as though it's something you drag around with you. It's not all of what you are, but it's part of you. The body and the mind are a unit."

Very interesting, I thought to myself. I had never considered the body and the mind as a unit. I was all ears as she continued with this new revelation.

"Specialized neural pathways that act as a bridge between the two, and whose function has gone largely unknown, are beginning to activate and strengthen in you. Both your hypothalamus, which is your second brain, and your pineal gland are complexes that act as conduits to the ethereal, and as they strengthen, you become receptive to higher electromagnetic energies. In addition, they will work in unison with your chakra centers to acclimate your body-mind to the quickened frequencies of a larger reality."

I understood the sister's words as she translated the language of the geometric transmission, which had no words of its own, but which directly imprinted information straight into my psyche—information that I was unable to hold on to as I received it. I didn't have the ability to hold onto it, and since there was no bridge leading back to its understanding, I used the sister's words as a bridge. Even though re-processing their meaning was the long way back, it was still easier than trying to access and interpret the initial imprints.

The difference between my method of processing through words rather than through a direct state of knowledge with imprints, was similar to the difference between the Wright Brother's first flight at Kittyhawk and the Starship Enterprise. This bothered me to no end, so I asked Sister Clementus about it.

"Salvatore, relax," she said, with a serene smile. "The Wright Brothers didn't start out with a 747 airliner. It was their intention of accomplishing flight that initiated an invisible process aimed at finding the means to do so. It may appear on the surface that this was formulated through exterior blueprints on paper, but that was not the case. At unseen levels, it was the power of their desirous intention that attracted the ethereal substances required to build the necessary interior pathways, which then externalized, and brought their manifestation to fruition.

"The same is true for you, too, my friend, but in a different way." She paused and seemed thoughtful for a moment. "Let me put it this way," she finally said. "A flux in consciousness is now quite evident in you because you have chosen to integrate with the concepts of a *higher octave* than the one you are accustomed to. New thought like this requires a longer integrative period. For you, it's an energetic oscillation across a larger-than-usual span. This balancing process in thinking, or vacillating between two systems of thought, is the cause of your forgetfulness. You are in a time of adjustment, and depending upon your focus, equalization will occur at some point within this span."

I had never thought of myself in such terms, but the sister had a compelling and reassuring confidence about her—nodding her head slowly, and smiling at me as she spoke, almost like a patient mother waiting for her child to swallow a mouthful of food before offering the next spoonful. Her explanation seemed to make perfect mathematical sense, but I related it more to machinery, or to an instrument of some kind.

"But you are an instrument!" she exclaimed.

I did another doubletake at her apparent ability to read my mind.

"Your senses, and the inner pathways you are strengthening, are instrumental in guiding you to what is true about you," she stated, unaffected by my awe at her extrasensory power.

"Could you explain more about the vibration of thought, then? I've always believed sound to be the only thing that vibrates. Yet, you're telling me that vibration has everything to do with what's true about me."

"Yes, gladly. I am well aware of your experience with the geometric transmission and I can't stress enough the importance of the fundamentals it imparted to you. Just remember that the Source of all life is the Highest Tone of Vibration. Everything in existence *is* vibration, and, extends from this Tone, which is The Great Spirit or THE WORD. There is simply nothing else. The more you know about your place in Creation in regard to the Source, the higher your tone, and the further you'll be on your evolutionary path," she declared in a clear, instructive voice, before placing her fingertips on her chest, and gazing upward on a slow, deep breath.

Her break allowed me a moment to contemplate on what she'd said, and I easily cross-referenced her words with the information brought forth by the geometrical language. When she appeared ready to resume our conversation, I asked with curious anticipation, "Sister, since we are extended from the Highest Tone, when you died, did you return to our Source?"

She shook her head. "No, I didn't. The natural laws of life don't work that way. Let me explain," she added with a patient smile on her face. "As splinters of light—from what can also be called the Eternal Light of Soul—death has no place in us. As a soul, I left this plane according to the principles of vibration, and with a certain level of frequency. At the time of my transition, I was drawn to a place of like-vibration where my evolution would be best served."

"I don't know what you mean by saying you transitioned to "like-vibration". Can you explain more fully?"

"It means that when a soul leaves earthly life, it magnetically attracts to where it needs to be in order to continue learning."

I nodded as comprehension set in. "Thank you, Sister. You make going to the next world sound so automatic."

"A soul's evolution is natural and ongoing," she said, matter-of-factly.

Before moving forward with questions our conversation stimulated in me, I thought about some of the pivotal moments of my life and wondered where I might find myself after leaving this world. I wanted to know if I should be aware of something specific that would benefit me in the hereafter. "What was the greatest lesson you learned?" I asked. "Was there one in particular that set you on the road to a higher level of understanding before your transition?"

"Indeed, there was," she blurted, clasping her hands together and pressing them against her chest as if she were eager to share. "Before I passed from my earthly experience of life, I learned that, similar to the way a ripple upon the water is part of its great ocean, so are we with our Source. When I began to grasp that ideology, however slightly, all other lessons proved to be further encompassments of the same thing.

"When we awaken to reality, the singularity principle of our Source is revealed. The awakening doesn't happen just because we *die*. It happens through an evolution in consciousness, or in other words, a tuning of our instrument. Likewise, your physical birth wasn't your creation, but a continuation. You are more than a body, yet you haven't risen to such awareness."

I was hypnotized by the words flowing from Sister Clementus' lips.

"Our purpose is not to blend with the Highest Tone, which, by natural law, is impossible because of our immeasurable difference in frequencies. We are only here to learn Its Laws. When you know the Law of Singularity, you will feel it with certainty, and like an inner honing device, it will guide you. Although we are not here to blend with the Source of all life, we, undoubtedly, are here to *know* of it, and to know how to live in harmony with Its Laws. This is what leads to every form of abundance."

I took her last comment to mean that *knowing* of singularity releases mental constriction and enables us to live to our highest potential. "Information like this isn't common. I mean— it's not something I learned in school or in church. Nothing of the kind has ever been presented to me," I said, feeling a sense of meekness flow through me.

"I have to disagree with you there, Salvatore. These things have been presented to you, but through the use of different words, and by people who didn't understand the depth of what they were saying. Religious leaders speak of Omnipresence, and in the next breath they warn of the possibility of separation from God. They literally *don't know* what they are talking about," she said, with a touch of embarrassment in her voice, since she herself was a leader in the physical world, I supposed.

"How do they get such a contradiction past the ears of their followers?" I asked.

"When the blind lead the blind, they speak the same language," she stated succulently.

My mind glazed over a bit at the metaphor.

"Salvatore, it's because the world hasn't awakened from its dream. The information I'm offering isn't the every-day-ness you're used to. If such were the case, many more souls, including you, would have evolved over the last millennium, and I wouldn't need to be here now," she said, while gliding her hands lightly over her forearms. "These types of hand movements help to keep my frequency high while I discuss the lower mindsets of your dimension," she explained at my curious frown. "Remember, I don't live here anymore," she added with a fleeting grin.

I allowed her the time to finish adjusting her frequency before I responded to her perplexing statement about the world's dreaming. "Sister, I don't understand what you meant when you said that the world hasn't awakened from its dream? I'm not dreaming, and neither are the people I know. We're all quite awake and mobile, and we aren't sleepwalking, either. So, what exactly are you trying to tell me?"

"I'm telling you that you have been dreaming, and for a very long time. I am here to help awaken you, Salvatore."

I looked at Sister Clementus, then at the three apparitions on the stairwell landing, all of whom were witnessing this scenario with me, but whom I'd almost forgotten were there because I'd been so focused on the Sister. The sound of silence was alarming. In light of the situation, I questioned if I was, in fact, dreaming all of this.

"No, you aren't home in bed sleeping and dreaming right now; and that is not the way you experience your worldly life, but you've been living in a *similar unreality*—one that breeds chaos. It has to do with how you see yourself, your perception of the world through that sense of self, and blind usage of the attributes innate to you since your creation. These are mistakes in need of correction, and that is all. This is a natural process, so don't be afraid. Be gladdened, for vision will be opened to you when you come out of blindness and learn to associate truth with what is real."

11

BEINGS FROM BEYOND BELIEF

"The quieter you become, the more you can hear."

— Ram Dass

I continued to understand most of what the Sister said to me, yet I still struggled with parts of the geometrical language. There hadn't been enough time for me to relax and fully absorb all the information I'd gotten while sitting on my hospital bed. The fact that the geometry could shed light on the reasons for confusion in the world came through to me; but without contemplation much of the transmission had already become vague. I could only hope that she would bring some clarity to the vagueness later on in our conversation.

Sister Clementus stood and slowly ran her palms down the sides of her shawl, three times. She placed her fingertips lightly on her chest, as she had done earlier, and with an upward gaze, she took a deep breath. Then, to my awe, she ascended slightly off the ground and intoned three long, heartfelt "OMs". After a moment of silence, she descended, apparently rejuvenated, and settled into what seemed to be a comfortable position. She caught and held my gaze as she resumed her lessons.

"The chaos of the world is evident all around you, Salvatore. But the truth is that it's not an absolute reality, even though it is experienced. The root of the chaos is that you live in a realm of perceived separation surrounded by degrees of intolerance. But let it be clear that *Intolerance is the result of people defining themselves by their differences,* while forgetting the most important thing: their *core unity.* People swing between the poles of various versions of "good and evil", and, "one's vice is another's virtue", while The Golden Rule of Life lay dormant on the back shelf of muddled minds; this debacle, generated by an incorrect sense of identity, is the dream of the world. Just like the dreams you have at night lose significance when you awaken in the morning, truth will unravel the seeming perpetual dream of every day life."

She gave me a few moments to sit quietly and absorb every word that came out of her mouth, and when she thought I was ready for more she recommenced.

"The best thing to do while living in your world of appearances is to use the information you are receiving to look within your mind, and practice attuning your thoughts to what is real." She stopped, tilted her head and gazed heavenward as if she were listening to someone, before facing me again. "Salvatore, the misperceptions of your third dimensional world promote the idea that eternity exists someplace far off in the future. Religions—that are yet to grasp the meaning of singularity—expose their error when proclaiming eternity to be dual with isolated places called heaven and hell. But the fact is that we are in eternity now. It's contradictory to think that there are two or more separate places in a unified field. Impossibilities like this can't exist in the Alpha and the Omega of life."

"That makes perfect sense to me, Sister, but why do so many people continue to believe what is impossible?"

"People see life in impossible ways and they remain stuck in impossibility because they *don't know what belief itself is*. They see the impossible, because they define themselves by the impossible in thinking that they can be isolated units of form. What's important to know here, is that since people are extensions of *All Power,* their thoughts are very powerful. When thoughts that are based on the belief in separation digress to conflicting differences, resistance is accumulated between them and becomes the root of strife."

As she talked about how belief led people to view life through impossibilities, I recalled that at a younger age, I used allegory to depict how we formulate our own personal realities. I saw everyone as projecting their thoughts onto the mirror of the world through filters of belief. The individual movies seen on the screen of each person's life made perfect sense to me, but because of life's distractions, I had a tendency to lose sight of these types of very important concepts, and so I didn't think about the dynamic of belief and projection regularly. Yet, I knew that forgetting about them had opened the door to digression, which led to conflict. I asked the sister how conflict and *falling asleep* in this way can be avoided.

"The conflict will stop when people learn that even though both the ego-personality and the body with their individual perceptions appear quite set and real, they are temporary, and should be used as mechanisms for awakening. You should not adhere to or defend them as your sole identity. When you come to know that which is real about you, belief in using differences as division devices will end, and appearances will be transformed. When we define ourselves by conflicting differences, we experience woe. What I'm telling you is highly significant and of great value, and especially deserving of your undivided attention," she said, as I overtly began vacillating.

"I have such an analytical mind, and I often need to stop and sift through everything you're conveying to me," I said by way of an apology.

"I wouldn't have appeared unless you were ready to receive it all. Just be patient as we go through the process," she said offering me a gentle, reassuring smile. When I nodded that I was ready, she continued. "You have been subjected to vast conflicts of differences in your life, too, Salvatore, especially concerning religion. Even now, detrimental instances that have been tucked away and forgotten, still have their effect on you."

The only thing I could relate to her comment was the time I spent following Jack and his congregation with their fearful beliefs. But their beliefs were no longer mine; however, her weighty reference had me thinking that maybe there was something else on her mind that was associated with my beliefs. Whatever it was, escaped me.

"It's important for you to understand, once and for all, that many of the scriptural interpretations proclaimed to be the truth by organized religion and its constituents, are erroneous. Religions cause much conflict in the world. It makes no difference who, or how many people follow them. Their grid of fearful projections, involving the personification of a devil and the possibility of separation from God, are but misunderstood metaphors running rampant between the poles of clarity and obscurity. The beliefs that tender this experience have no validity in themselves, except to show their own dynamic coloring of perception. This means that beliefs are secondary to you, and as such, can never define you."

Sister Clementus was reinforcing what the ancient mystics have taught throughout time: false beliefs create false appearances, and project them onto the screen of life, but—like dreams—they do not truly exist.

"When core beliefs begin to gravitate toward the positive pole of Spirit, the vacillation produced between the old beliefs, and the new, actually serves to depolarize old paradigms. This process leads to a profound shift in consciousness, and when it occurs, we will no longer live in accordance with the appearances generated by blind belief, but by what is real. We achieve this outcome by interfacing the lower self and its projected false belief, with the higher self and its extension of truth."

Temporarily, satisfied with my lesson on the perils of false beliefs, I asked, "Can you tell me more about our identity as beings of light, Sister?"

"We are all beings of light, emanating from a Greater Light," she began, her smiling face portraying her unusual willingness to oblige. "But through fascination with the reflection of our own makings, we slipped into hypnosis and forgot our freedom in the neutrality of Creation."

"But how could we do such a thing?" I asked in wonder.

"The only way we could have found ourselves in such a circumstance was through innocence. The Garden of Eden metaphor was about early, pristine mind, which, by definition, had no experience or frame of reference to draw from. We were free, but didn't yet know freedom's meaning, and so we turned its gifts into burdens. The law of creation was unknowingly used in reverse when we assigned power to our manifestations and allowed them to rule. But our manifestations have no power of their own since they do not truly exist in the absolute sense. That which we perceive as powerful within them, is merely a transference of our own power that has culminated into what you see in the world today. Life is fluid, and not meant to be frozen in projected thought forms."

"Can you expound on projected thought forms? Also, can you show me from another angle how we reversed the law of creation?" I asked, not quite sure what she meant. "I mean, can we actually do that?"

"I'll answer your last question first. No, the universal laws are immutable, and they cannot be reversed, but they are neutral and can be used in an inverted way. Now, to your first question: awareness fell asleep when we began masking reality with wrong beliefs about our identities, and as we continued to step farther into our projected thought-forms, we became like dreamers, lost in dreams. Our holy nature—as extensions of Perfection—was forgotten. Becoming blind to our core identity is the original, and, only sin."

"It seems to me that freedom has gotten us into a lot of trouble, so I don't understand why there is so much freedom with the laws," I said with a little hesitance.

The Sister looked at me with confused patience before expounding on the topic of freedom. "We are free because we are facets of a neutral universe. There is no authority in the way humans think of it. There are only universal principles that are always in effect. Although judgment is never cast upon us, freedom comes with responsibility. *The universe is just*; therefore, we reap the justice of our thoughts, words, and actions unto ourselves. No separate "God Being" does anything to you. You do it to yourselves and amongst yourselves. People only act in accordance with what they know at any given time."

Sister Clementus' last statement caused me to relate the symbol of the serpent to man's lower self as it goes through life—limited to moving in one trajectory—based on its belief in separation, yet actually going nowhere. Her next response to my unasked question told me she'd read my mind again.

"The serpent portrays man's displaced sense of identity and its 'stuck-in-repetition' situation. It is the chattering fragment of mind that is reactive and usurps awareness of the present moment, as it distracts us from who we truly are."

"Is this the same serpent that tempted Eve in the Garden of Eden, and also Jesus at Gethsemane?"

"Yes. But remember, we are dealing with allegory in this regard. There was no actual reptile involved. The allegory demonstrates how our pre-human state misunderstood the workings of its own consciousness, because of our innocence while in the garden of life. Even Jesus struggled with that aspect of mind at Gethsemane; yet, he overcame it through attracting knowledge of his own being to himself. Yes, he was a Son of God, but so is everyone else. Jesus was referred to as *The* Son, because he aligned himself perfectly with The Universal Intelligence and evolved to a fully realized being. This is what it means to be Christed. The purpose of humanity is to evolve to *know thyself* as Jesus did, which is exactly what he taught. No one can see this truth while drawing from the limited frame of reference that humanity has been duplicating onto the screen of life for millenniums."

The sister suddenly stopped talking, stood up, and took a few steps away from me. With her feet together and her palms touching above her head, she looked straight ahead. She inhaled deeply and slowly, then she exhaled immediately and held her breath out for five seconds, then inhaled and exhaled, holding her exhalation out for five seconds again. She repeated this breathing process nine times.

I felt blessed to be in her sparkling presence, and while observing her, I found myself automatically breathing in a similar fashion. I waited until she gracefully returned to her seat beside me, before I asked my next question. "Sister, I realize you've already explained it, but could you please show me another way people can stop duplicating limitation onto the screen of life?"

"Salvatore, I can continue to show you in a thousand different ways, but I can assure you, they all point to the same process of evolution. In order to stop the duplication, it is required that people be still and ask these questions of themselves: *What is my identity, or not my identity, as a universal being? What are the dynamics of belief, and what is perception?*"

Everything Sister Clementus said rang through me like new life. It didn't matter what angle she used to get her point across, they all led to one basic understanding: clarity about the meaning of *Living by the Spirit instead of by the letter*, as described by the Apostle Paul in the Bible. I understood both the scripture, and the sister's explanation to mean that we should live according to the God of our hearts and rise above the words of any religion. Her insights also illuminated the idea that when we begin to question the fundamentals of human consciousness—such as: identity, belief, and perception—we attract to ourselves higher frequencies of thought. She referred to this type of questioning as *the food of enlightenment.*

I had so much more to ask her, and so much more to learn. "Sister, since everything is unified, does this mean that there's no evil power, like the devil, that's disconnected from what we call God?"

"I'm glad you asked that question, since the answer is very meaningful. The metaphor of the devil is true. First of all, it must be realized that evil stems from ego, and, that it has no essence in the cosmic. There aren't two opposing Beings somewhere in space —one good and one evil. The *sin of pride*, which started the idea of separation from The Universal Intelligence, is actually about the clinging to a limited sense of identity. Calling the mistake a lie, implies that it was done to us, and that there could be blame directed somewhere, which is not the case. That particular mistake, which we call *the father of lies*, is one of our own making. The mistake duplicated itself in the mirror of the world through then unknown mechanisms of the mind. This is why we lost the *sense* of our true identity as sons and daughters created in the image and likeness of Pure Spirit. As paradoxical as it sounds, the truth is that it was all meant to be as part of our involution and our evolution.

"In their mistaken belief concerning identity, people become blinded, and as a result they acquire a sense of incompleteness in identification with an ego-personality. But that cannot change the truth of what they truly are. The problem is that in their blindness, most still don't know what they have done."

The sister was adamant as she explained that it was only our sense of identity that was lost, not our identity itself, and I became more enthralled by the facts she imparted to me.

"Spiritual beings are the *breath of life* emanating from *undefined infinite light energy*, but due to millenniums of blind thinking, they learned to define themselves by their projected beliefs, instead. But Absolute Reality holds the mystery of our identity, Salvatore, which means, *we are from beyond belief.*"

"I look forward to the day when the world will see beyond the projected world of appearances," I said.

"You can do that now. You only need to step aside from your conditioned thinking and, from an angle, perceive where you can appraise the reactive behaviors of history for what they are. That is the way of true vision. There, you will begin self-realization beyond what your five senses tell you, and then the *Law of Use* will be set before you so that you can extend this realization to others."

"The Law of Use?"

"Yes. When you know the truth, you must use it to the benefit of others. On the contrary, exclusion of others is a misguided mental function stemming from convoluted ideas that leads to the belief in inequality. Ego projections on the screen of the world cannot divide Spirit, but their crafty purveyors come equipped with psychological defense mechanisms geared to keep divisiveness intact."

"But why would anyone defend what isn't real?"

"Because it appears real to them. They believe that a compilation of experiences that they call "a personality" is all of who they are, not knowing that the ego-personality is not a true identity at all, but a perceptual tool that has been psychologically displaced and misused. The ego—our lens on life—is best used as a sounding board to help humanity understand the workings of perception, which, when understood, will direct them toward the positive pole of Spirit. Without knowledge of Spirit, a blind ego will go so far as to kill the body, as we've all witnessed in the ways of the third-dimensional world. But we are souls, and spiritual discernment shows us that the soul can never die. Nonetheless, *the reality that exclusion from the Oneness of Life cannot happen*, doesn't stop man-made theologies from projecting belief in alienation onto the face of Omnipresence. Those who adhere to the latter way of thinking prolong time by stalling in repetition, like shadows looking for light, but lost in a roomful of mirrors."

12

THE FALSE IS THE DEAD

"Our scientific power has outrun our spiritual power. We have guided missiles and misguided men."

— Martin Luther King, Jr.

The sister's endless plethora of knowledge helped me to understand more about the maligned perception of the world, which I now saw as a compounded effect of repetitive, misaligned thinking. For thousands of years, common perception has been blindly filtered by dense egoic mindsets; but when thought transference, and the belief projecting dynamic of perception itself, is understood, the cause of the malignancy becomes apparent. From this overview, perception is no longer viewed as external reality, and instead becomes a steppingstone, pointing toward whatever manner of thought is within ourselves.

I was learning, yet, I needed to fully examine this way of thinking until I gained a high level of certainty. In order to accomplish that goal, I needed to continue to pick the sister's brain, but my inquiry was temporarily put on hold when, without warning, my translucent friend arose from the bench and without uttering a word, led me toward The Gospel Lighthouse Church.

When people walk, there's rhythm to their gait, but since she floated on air, there was none to her movement; I found it quite fascinating, even as I reveled in the idea that we would enter the church, and that the sister would share her wisdom with its members. With much disappointment, I soon discovered that there would be no such occurrence. As I moved closer to the door, I was startled at the feeling of repulsion that overtook me. Then, to my surprise, Sister Clementus addressed me in a firm voice.

"Salvatore, due to your gradual awakening, the frequency of your vibration has quickened, and as a result, you've become uncomfortable and hesitant to enter the church. The people inside haven't yet grown enough to be truly attuned to Spirit. Their vibration is dissonant to yours because their life experiences are still deeply entrenched in third-dimensional thinking. They judge and condemn because they continue to eat from the tree of the knowledge of good and evil."

Her words were inspiring, but I still grimaced at the Pastor's exhortations about heaven and hell filtering through the door, and at the congregation's emotional outbursts as the organist played to the choir. Images of the ever-brittle church Elder, Suzanne, came to mind, as did unpleasant thoughts about the coldness of the women with the beehive hairdos. But it was the thought of Sandy, having some kind of mental breakdown, that caused me to shudder and turn away now, just as it had done in the past. I was at a loss for the meaning of *Eating from the tree of the knowledge of good and evil,* so of course, once we returned to the comfort of our place on the grass, I asked the sister to enlighten me.

"I'm gratefully obliged to help," she said. "But the answer to your question is in everything we've already discussed. The allegory states that there was no *good* or *bad* until we blindly formulated them into ideas, by unknowingly planting a seed of impossibility while we existed in our pure and fertile consciousness in the Garden of Eden. The seed was the initial belief in our disconnection from everything, including our Source. Such a belief demonstrates an inferior identity—one that constructs subsequent identities by flipping to the other side of the same coin to fabricate a sense of superiority. This false belief manifests in degrees—from the actions of bullies and mainstream religions, all the way to those who will kill, steal, and destroy, to protect the mistake they see as themselves. They behave in this revolting way because they don't know that they already have everything they need. When we act from that initial, incorrect belief—or the original sin—we're eating from the tree of the knowledge of good and evil."

I pondered on her simplification of *eating from the tree of the knowledge of good and evil* for a few seconds before responding. "I deeply appreciate your complete explanation, Sister, yet it gives rise to more questions."

"Go on," she prompted with a boosting smile.

I took a deep breath. "Since the world has been based on such misperception, could we say that the error opened the way for the manifestation of a... sort of *sub-creation*, perhaps?"

"Yes," she exclaimed, nodding and smiling like a teacher whose student had finally gotten the point. "The sub-creation is a projection of the lie that has been spread throughout the world for ages. The truth is that we are all a part of One Life— aspects of the One Mind—yet most people have not awakened to this most basic reality. A simple formula to help you remember this truth is to *bring the One to the Two—Singularity to Plurality*. It's a formula of Universal Principle that reveals the truth that there's no division between you, even though it may appear so. If people were fully conscious of this verity, it would be the end of all mistakes—the end of religion's definition of sin, and the end of the common perception of death. If you were to see clearly, you would know the difference between what is true, real, and eternal, and what is false, illusory, and temporal experiences."

"Well, now that's a huge shift in perception. I appreciate your simple choice of words," I said, while holding tightly to the gist of her elucidation. "But would you please expand my cognition as to why the world continues to perpetuate the original mistake in such a manner, Sister?"

"Most certainly. When they are unaware of the laws of perception, people generally project their thoughts outward, and then misinterpret the reflected images of those same thoughts as having external origins. When you misunderstand reality as being external—functioning independently of the beliefs feeding your thoughts—you remain asleep and robotic in the light of Creation. Dear, Salvatore, one day, people will know that they aren't just meat-bodies living in external realities disconnected from the Great Light, or what they call, *God*."

"Thank you so much for shedding light on these truths, Sister. I just find it incredibly paradoxical that there is so much violence in the world, inflicted on certain groups by others, when we are all electromagnetically bound together."

"A very insightful observation. We are united by, and, of one invisible substance at the core, otherwise there would be no UNIverse. Humanity struggles against the compounding network of conflicting thought-forms it has blindly formulated and projected onto the screen of life. But humanity's reactive attacks on itself only perpetuate the illusion and hide the truth. In such chaos, the only sane function of humanity is to correct misperception so it can expose its dreaming. Only then, will light shine through the thin walls of so-called separate identities with their belief in the false—which is dead."

The sister's equation of the *false* with the *dead* drove me to deeper levels of thought. I could only surmise that such illusory dreaming was the root of evil. "Is there something we can do to fight evil in the world?" I asked.

"You are correct in thinking that evil is based in the illusory dreams of the world, but you must understand that evil has no power, except for the power people assign to it. When you engage in a struggle against what you see as external evil, you define it as an autonomous force, when it is not. Evil tends to be viewed as a separate energy when it is actually a projection of derelict mindsets. Though at times it is necessary to protect one's self, violence only begets more violence, so evil must be addressed at the core."

"Surely, you don't deny, in any way, that there's evil in the world, Sister!"

"No, Salvatore, I don't. But it's not just *out there*, in and of itself. In order to affect evil, people need to look within themselves at the way they use their own thoughts. So many people hold onto religious beliefs that dress evil with fear, involving the personifications of Satan and his army of demons, when *satanas* is but a Greek word that means *adversary.*"

"Now you're scaring me, Sister. I thought you said there was no devil."

She gave me an affectionate smile like a teacher would give a curious student who'd asked an innocent, yet obvious question. "You're scaring yourself. The only adversary you're up against is ignorance of your true identity. This goes for all of humanity. When this ignorance waxes, it continues to attract energy like itself, which becomes evident when it grows in negativity to the horrors you call evil. The root of evil is the self-centered, self-serving, and unchecked thinking of people who are disconnected from knowing Spirit."

Wow! That was a truckload of truth to help put a damper on some serious scriptural misinterpretations. I grew more curious and anxious to learn more, so I asked, "Could you give me an example of how people who are disconnected from knowing Spirit, might think?"

"Any way of thinking that brings harm to one's self or to others. Is that simple enough for you, Salvatore?" she asked with a sliver of humor in her voice.

I chuckled inside, treasuring the way she simplified many ideas by corralling them into one. On a more serious note, I thought about instances when I'd felt hurt by the things particular people had said and done to me, and vice-versa. From what I'd learned so far from the sister, it became evident that everything we think, say, and do, is always based in whatever paradigms, or models of behavior ruled the society at those specific times. The sister's depiction of evil had sunk in quite solidly, but I wanted to gain as much wisdom as possible about the subject. And without my even asking out loud, she responded to my thoughts.

"You say you want to fight evil, Salvatore, but in the dual nature of perception that's in line with humanity's stage of evolution, change happens in another way. In a world that believes in opposites as divisions when divisions don't exist at the core of life-energy, change can only happen when you learn to *use your illusions* —rather than through fighting them," she uttered in a louder than usual tone before growing quiet.

From her bowed head and pensive expression, I assumed that the sister needed time to reflect on what she had said, so I used the break to mentally revisit the subjects of opposites we'd already spoken about: hot and cold, happy and sad. I realized that their duality is not separate, just different degrees of the same thing. I didn't entirely understand where she was going with this, but it was easy to conclude that it was illusory to see opposites as two divided parts. But how do we use illusions to affect evil? Thoughts along this line left me blank, so I did what she expected me to do.

"Sister," I began in a humbled spirit, "I feel like I've hit a brick wall. I'm at a loss as to what you mean by using illusions to cause an impact on the idea of evil." My intellectual stake in this was vast, so every receptive organ in me waited earnestly for her answer.

"Keep it simple, Salvatore. Begin by remembering that all your thoughts and emotions rise out of the same core-energy. Although you color thoughts with your interpretations of life experiences, those thoughts are not your identity. Your task is to attune your mind's eye to the singularity of the core energy that permeates everything."

"But I already know that, Sister!" I persisted, somewhat disappointed in her response. "This is what I want to know: what does using illusions have to do with dealing with evil?"

"I'm well aware that you know, Salvatore. What I asked is that you *remember* certain very important principles. So I must direct you to relax and be patient while I give you the rest of my answer."

Her counter was gentle, yet firm. I felt embarrassed by my sudden over-zealousness. "Please forgive me, Sister. I lost a grip on my enthusiasm. After the lurid experiences I've had involving the duality of heaven and hell, I want nothing more than to understand opposites and duality. I know I must slow my mind in order to be receptive, and I will, so please excuse me."

"I'm aware of your experiences with religion, so your reaction was perfectly normal, and expected, Salvatore. In light of everything we've discussed, do you honestly think you need to beg forgiveness of me?"

I breathed a sigh of gratitude that she understood and could be so readily forgiving. I felt comforted in her love and her kindness. But when she suddenly embraced me, I felt instantaneously elevated to a serene, higher frame of mind from where I became more receptive. She stood behind me and placed both hands on the top of my head for about three minutes. I felt as if I was enveloped in a soft, yet constant wind, blowing down from above my head, through my body, and out the soles of my feet. While I was experiencing those unfamiliar, yet calming sensations in my body, she dragged her palms from the sides of my neck to my outer shoulders, three times, as though brushing away dust. I instantly felt like a brand new being.

"May I proceed, now?" she asked, gentleness and patience emanating from her aura to mine.

"Yes, please do," I replied, surprised at the passiveness in my voice and being.

"Good. Now, I also want you to remember that it's the simplest of thoughts that can grow in negativity, even across life-times. So, when you have a negative thought, don't struggle with it. The law of life says we reap what we sow, which in this case means, directing energy into resisting a thought only reinforces it. This is a lower natural law. Through the use of your will, you have the ability to use the higher laws of life over the lower laws to affect change."

I was intrigued! This was the part of the geometrical language I'd been unable to grasp while I was in the hospital because it had begun to dissolve at that time. "What are the higher laws, Sister, and what is meant by the idea of using higher laws over lower laws?" I asked, as my heart pounded with anticipation.

"The higher laws involve using the vibration of thought as an effective tool of change. This is done in a nonresistant way. Instead of becoming caught up in resisting what you want to change, acknowledge it, as well as every emotion attached to it. Do this, without judgment, from a neutral zone. Then, focus your thinking on its opposite. For example, if you want to omit smoking cigarettes from your life, the effective tool to use would be to think about fresh air—a lot! But the catch here is to add the *catalyst of emotion*. You must fall in love with fresh air, every day, throughout the day. Taste it, feel it, and enjoy it thoroughly. In doing so, you are using Harmonic Law by infusing higher thought vibration into lower thought vibration. The higher will raise the lower. The result is that you've changed the degree of your experience between the opposite poles of breathing air to where you want it. This is one scenario of mastering your thoughts, instead of allowing them to master you."

A barrage of dichotomies surfaced in my mind. I could see that I would get lots of practice changing the degrees of polarity in many areas of my thinking, simply by evoking the catalyst of emotion to infuse higher thought into lower thought. I hoped I could actually do it. The prospect thrilled me. I knew there were areas in my life where it was plain that my thoughts did, indeed, rule me. I asked the sister about this.

"The reason you feel as though your thoughts control you is that, like most people, you've defined yourself by them, at least in some areas of your life experience. You will reach a point where you understand that your thoughts can never define you, nor should you allow them to. None of that old way of thinking is true. What is true, is that you still haven't fully learned how to define yourself, nor do you know what you are not."

I felt as if the sister was right on target to some degree, but when she said that I still didn't know how to define myself, it made me realize that when we discussed using these laws to create change for the better, we weren't just talking about mundane things—like quitting smoking, goal-setting, or turning a sad day into a happy day. What was being conveyed to me included those issues, of course, but the all-inclusiveness of the Law crossed all octaves, applying not only to the transformation of those small things, but also to the transforming of our identity, the identity of our planet, and of the entire universe. So, obviously, if I wasn't seeing it working in one section of my life, such as where I believed my thoughts controlled me, then I wasn't seeing it at all.

"What's most important right now, Salvatore, is that, like an antenna, your attitude is set at an angle to receive, and you have been receiving, haven't you?" she asked skeptically.

"There's no doubt that's true, Sister." I assumed it was obvious to both of us that I was receiving. She suggested that I continue to relax and allow for the process to continue. I still wanted to know more about the method of working with thought-energy. But with so much oscillation around the topic of dichotomies, I wasn't sure where to begin. "Does this mean that love and hate are opposite poles of a sameness?" I asked, giving it a go, anyway.

"No, it doesn't," she said with raised eyebrows. "Love, as the natural glue that holds all life together, is in a higher octave. It transcends the world of opposites. You are equating love with *desire*, whose opposite is *disappointment*. Hate comes about through compounded incorrect thinking that pertains to the latter. What's important in dealing with such emotional opposites is to know that as electromagnetic beings and directors of electromagnetic energy, we can reinterpret feelings of disappointment. We can raise our thinking to a higher octave to where the deprivation of division is transcended. Then, the higher laws can be applied to affect change. This *mental alchemy* circumvents conflict, and, is the key to the profound. It has the power to transform the world. *But there is one prerequisite.*"

"And, what is that?"

"A correct view of yourself as the evolving, universal being that you are. A knowing of where to base, or, where not to base your sense of identity. There are many exercises to help awaken this knowing, such as focusing your attention on the life force in your body. You have already practiced these methods in the teachings of your mystery school. Continue in this way, as the mystics have much more to show you."

She was right. For months I had been practicing the art of attuning to, and strengthening what was referred to as my *psychic body*. All of these practices were tools used to raise my frequency of vibration and acclimate the subtle mechanisms of my physicality to the ethereal, which, ultimately led to the awareness of a Greater Whole, and to a higher degree of understanding the soul.

"Although you cannot fully understand the Greater Whole at this time, it's enough to know the law of truth, which is that you are more than just connected to all people in some way. The law of the universe says that they are actually a part of you. No man is an island. To not realize this most basic universal principle and operate in the world through a sense of separation leads to disappointment, simply because you were never appointed to separation—which you know is impossible, since we've already discussed it. This disappointment causes a sense of a void in you, when, in reality, there cannot be one. If this sense of incompleteness is not correctly appraised, it can digress to evil and the use of thought to the detriment of others, which, in return, brings more woe."

I stood enraptured soaking up the sister's generous intellect as the warmth of the light radiating from her filled me.

"When you realize the true way of life, you'll see the light within you shine as the same light in others," she continued, after obviously reading my last thought. "All will be revealed through a raising of global consciousness, when time and its counterpart of perception as you know it ends. You will move beyond perception and into *knowledge*, which is past the five organic senses of the body. You will see the profundity of your unity when you finally come to know that you are *All One Life.*"

"Amen," I declared, hoping that the day would truly arrive when we all move into *knowledge*.

Sister Clementus moved closer and asked me to stand. When I did, she proceeded to tap her hands and fingers firmly up and down the meridians of my body for approximately three minutes. She rested her hands on my scalp, for what seemed like five minutes, during which time electricity flowed lightly through me. Then from all angles, she whisked her hands downward from my head to my waist. She did the same to my arms, hands, and legs, briskly moving toward the ground.

When she was finished with me, I watched, in an aura of calm, as she self-cleansed by moving effortlessly in what appeared to be a Tai Chi dance. I was familiar with Tai Chi, so I knew that her graceful hand motions were the methods used to pull chi into her being, and move old energy out and into the ground. When she was done, I thanked her and we rested for a few more moments in our newly refreshed state before engaging in more discussion.

"I can sense that we are All One beneath our misperceptions, Sister," I said, breaking the silence. "This sense has opened me up to the idea that humanity has been distracted by its use of words. Words seem to have constricted people, and many things about life into labels."

She graced me with an amicable smile. "There's no need to continue to call me Sister Clementus. When I lived in the physical dimension, my birth name was Gloria. It's a lovely name, but I stopped using it after my final vows as a nun. I'd like you to use it now."

"Alright, Gloria, I will. I quite like the name, too," I added, smiling back at her.

She dipped her head in appreciation of my compliment then got right back on course. "Now that we're refreshed and invigo-rated, let's talk about words. Unaware that words are names, signs, and symbols used as representations, humans over-identify with them in the physical dimension. For example, when people define themselves by an assigned name, which is then attached to a phys-ical human body that ages and dies, they're seeing themselves only superficially. They don't see their wholeness. You are partly a material body that, like all matter, is subject to laws, and that is in a constant state of change, leading to decay. But what you don't see, is the *Essence* of matter, the essence of the life being expressed through it. You see your life as a body with a short span of existence when the truth is that Endless Life animates you. It may surprise you to hear that the time is coming when even your physical body will be immortal. You don't know this fact because you only see from your current level of development, or from what you've been conditioned to believe."

"Actually, I have been taught about such things, Gloria. But I've only reached a point in my understanding that involves more conceptualization, rather than the direct knowing of them. What else can be seen when looking at a human being? And how can I see it?" I asked.

"Concepts come before the understanding of knowledge, but for you, it comes in the natural order of your awakening. As far as whatever else can be seen when considering a human being, some things are indefinable in words. Since all symbolic representations, such as words, are crystallized thoughts set aside for viewing, words can't help being degrees removed from the reality of what is represented."

"A statement hard for me to comprehend. Can you give me another example I can understand? Maybe something a little more concrete to satisfy my simple eye?"

"You have complicated what truly is simple," she said softly, while lightly gliding her palms together as though she were preparing to pray. "Using the human organism as the end result, think of what you see as your physical body in terms of its levels of organization."

I understood the levels of the human organism, so I rattled them off with a sense of pride. "Before the human organism comes organ systems, organs, tissue, cells, molecules, and atoms, first—right?"

"Yes. Now, go further, and look more closely at atomic structure. You will see protons, neutrons, and electrons actively exchanging electrical charges like little lightning bolts." Gloria placed her left hand on her right shoulder and her right hand on her left shoulder, in what was known by the mystics as a position of supplication.

As I observed her, I gasped aloud when I became over-whelmed by a physical sensation that I could only equate to an accordion being compressed. It blew my mind when I realized that Gloria had somehow shrunk me, or had perhaps placed my consciousness inside an atom of my body.

"Look closer still at the vibrating components of light—all with a great relative distance between them. Do you see anything solid there?" she asked, excitedly.

I was breathless while trying to process the beauty of the light around me which seemed to go on forever. I couldn't immediately grasp that this was inner, and not outer space. It was a stark reminder of the extent to which my senses were habitually focused outward. "Well, no!" I cried. "I don't see anything solid. Am I looking in the wrong place?"

"No, you're not. There really is no such thing as solidity," she said, pointedly. "You live in a world of appearances, or representa-tions and names for things that don't exist the way you think they do."

Her answer lay heavy on my mind, but her next question made perfect sense.

"Now that you've looked toward the infinite microcosm starting with the human organism, isn't it fitting that you look toward the macrocosm in the same way?"

I took a deep breath. My high school days came to mind, and I recalled the abstract image of a man's face and the words, "Man, A Complex Being", encased in a silver frame hanging on the cafeteria wall. Also, the obviously incomplete evolutionary chart in my science class had me thinking, *Why would man's evolution end, just because he stood upright?*

13

ONE SIN, ONE SOLUTION

"Conscience never deceives us and is the true guide of humanity. She is to the soul what instinct is to the body; whoever follows her pursues the direct path of nature and need not fear being misled."

— Jean Jacques Rousseau

The feeling of being blown up like a balloon seemed unending when Gloria macro-cosmically expanded my consciousness. I had to hold onto the thought that this involved only my consciousness, not my physicality, which made me realize, once again, the point to which I had limited my perception to my body and its five senses throughout my life. She quickly guided me farther through what seemed like infinite boundlessness so I only got fleeting glimpses of our solar system and The Milky Way Galaxy as we traveled. What I saw now, was as extraordinarily beautiful as what I'd seen in the microcosm, and with surprise, I came to realize that the microcosm and macrocosm were the same, just viewed from different perspectives.

Gloria brought me abruptly back and gave me time to absorb

what I had experienced before she explained our short voyage into the infinite regions of the universe.

"Salvatore, it was your consciousness that I used for the process to take place. One day, when you learn Mastery over the elements, you will be able to do the same thing, and even much more. You will grow to understand that everything in your midst is a dance of electromagnetic exchanges, vibrating at various frequencies of which the physical dimension and your organic sensory faculties are a composite. Contemplate that everything coming through your five senses is based on the workings of an orderly Grand Cosmic Scale. You are part of this order, but what's more life-changing is that you are awakening to your natural power to create within it."

"Gloria, I hear you say these things, but I still don't understand how it all works, how everything comes together. You make it sound so simple. But it's not simple to me."

"I understand your inability to grasp it all. But you must consider that you're in the integrative period of this learning."

"Thanks for understanding, Gloria. I promise to do the best I can with the intricacies of what you convey."

"You'll be fine. As you gather bits and pieces of knowledge, you will see how everything eventually comes together. May I continue?" she asked, politely.

"Please," I said, with a tentative grin.

"Although your body was cast from the dust of the earth, its elemental essence is generated by light from beyond the atomic level in all things. The gaseous exchanges that occur during respiration bring oxygen to your body and eliminate waste. But it's the positive and negative polarities of the Vital Life Force in the air you breathe, and in the food you eat, that bring life to the cell nucleus and membrane, respectively, by way of the circulatory system. This results in an electromagnetic field between the two, creating the cell as the basic unit of life. Life is in the blood, Salvatore. The Creator of ALL LIFE breathes into your body." Gloria tipped her head slightly forward while gazing earnestly at me. "Are you now beginning to realize there is much more to you than what you know?"

"I think I need more time than most people to process these types of things," I said, feeling a bit shy.

She leaned in closer, and asked in a softer tone, "Do you like music?"

"I quite like music," I replied with enthusiasm.

"What do you like about it?"

"Its soothing effect, and its power to lift me emotionally. Why do you ask?"

"Because I want to show you something about the Principles of Vibration." She straightened up. "Music is sound, and sounds are obvious rates of vibration. When you look at the mathematics of music, you will understand there is harmony when keys vibrate together at wavelengths with a distinct frequency differential.

"Light is also vibration. The physiology of the ear is sensitive to the vibrations of sound, and the cones and rods of the human retina receive the much higher vibrations of light. Notice that there are seven keys of audible sound and seven colors in the visible light spectrum, which are complementary by Harmonic Law, according to their rates of vibration; evidence of a universal order is demonstrated by these laws. When you attune to music or art, it calibrates your body, your mind, and your emotions to this order, and you can feel it."

I recalled seeing a demonstration of shards of metal on a plate forming distinct geometrical designs when tones of the musical scale vibrated the plate. I listened with profuse interest as Gloria continued.

"Think of life as though it were music, knowing that the word *spirit* means breath, or *wind,* and the word *universe* means *one song.* We are all intrinsic parts of a highly vibrating wind song, and we have the choice to either be in tune with the music, or to suffer the chaos of noise. Either way, everything is part of the great wind song of life—a song with an incomprehensible composer. Knowledge like this can only be appreciated when you learn to still your overactive surface mind and listen from within."

A smile cracked my lips. "The beauty in your metaphor is that I think I'm beginning to understand it, Gloria."

"I'm describing facts about reality. You are a part of reality; therefore, everything I've told you is already within you. What you think you're beginning to understand is more about recognizing what you already know—otherwise, you wouldn't be able to hear it."

I could only shake my head and chuckle at the revelation that everything she was teaching me was already part of me. Remarkable!

Gloria smiled at my astonishment and then continued. "Another aspect of the law is that thought vibrations attract their own likeness, and due to our shared essence, all people, as part of the Thought of God, resonate in what is called *agape*—the inborn love we have for one another. But people are largely blinded to this love as they live cloaked in circumventing beliefs about their identity, which is either sleeping in the lower levels of ego, or based in an expanded perspective."

"I think what I hear you saying is that people are of two minds. Isn't this a kind of *split-personality?*"

"Yes, it is, but on a larger scale than how you would ordinarily use the term. The one sin, which is about the splitting of the mind, is always the same. As extensions of our Creator, we are unified, and have all the Creator's attributes. We are all like little duplicates of God with the ability to create. Yet, humanity has not fully awakened to its innate attributes, let alone their uses."

When I heard Gloria say, "Humanity has not fully awakened...", I told her that I recalled hearing about the words, *Know*

Thyself, written upon the entrance to the Temple of Apollo in ancient Greece.

"Salvatore, most people know nothing of the unified field of life, much less their function in it. I implore you to understand that thought is creative energy, and that such ignorant thought in people *creates in a trajectory after its own limitation.* As an offshoot of this foundational error, humans have formulated a false identity, as I've previously explained. I want to make it clear to you that, in a way, this so-called identity thinks it has *mentally* split itself off from the immutable—the unified field. But in reality, the split did not and cannot happen or exist—yet it can be *experienced,* which is not the same as existence. The time will come when all will discover that from the *eyes* of a higher dimension, there is really only One Mind in all of us, and we in IT. This realization is the Golden Key, the greatest step of humanity, which will expand the *perception* of life to the *knowledge* of life."

The more she spoke, the more boggled my mind became. I was about to ask a question when she raised a finger to stop me, then stood back from me as she'd previously done.

This time, with her feet spread apart and her hands at her sides with palms facing upward, she went into another breathing exercise. She slowly inhaled and exhaled, this time holding her breath for about five seconds at the end of each inhalation. She performed this technique nine times. When she returned her attention to me, I noticed a new glow about her. She sat beside me, and we remained quiet for a few minutes before she nodded for me to proceed.

"How can there be just one mind?" I asked her. "Sometimes I think I understand what you mean by *One Mind,* then at other times I lose focus, just like I do when I think about the possibility of the existence of other dimensions."

"The One Mind of which I speak isn't the same as your brainy mind with all its disquieting ramblings, my dear Salvatore.

Here's a relevant exercise that you can try later on: Sit comfortably and notice your thoughts. As they stream along, practice acknowledging them without indulging in them. Be in the present moment using your breath as an anchor. Without strain, direct your attention to the space between your thoughts. This is the realm of the One Mind in which your thoughts move. With practice, you'll notice how the place between your thoughts is quiet. Then, as you continue to practice *as an observant witness,* you'll begin to identify more with what's between your thoughts than with the thoughts themselves. This touches on what is true about you, and it's also one avenue towards understanding that you are a *Thought in the Mind of God.* In fact, when you stop giving your chattering thoughts power, you will come to see everything around you differently as they move through this space."

To my amazement, I realized that I had already been practicing this exercise on my own for years and, without anyone teaching me. Learning this practice at a young age had proven to be a pivotal point in my life. It had opened a doorway to another part of me, a part that was clairvoyant and, that had allowed me to engage in out-of-body-experiences. I was thrown by the fact that Gloria used the term, *The place between your thoughts,* because that's the same term I'd used in regard to this practice. Gloria looked at me and grinned. I could tell that she knew I was familiar with this ritual. It was as though she was acknowledging and reinforcing that it was a very important ritual to practice.

"Thinking in terms of dimensions, Salvatore, recall the ones you're familiar with. For example: length, height, and width. These are called *dimensional planes.* Compare the slower vibrations of tangible material objects to the inaudible frequencies of sound, and to the imperceptibility of higher frequencies of light, such as ultraviolet. When you start thinking on the level of electromagnetism and frequency of vibration, you will begin to comprehend how they are intrinsic to dimensional planes—

including invisible ones that are right here among us. This can be used as a starting point for understanding the viability of multidimensionality.

"Perception of separation is the root of the illusory split, and it is fostered by people incorrectly defining themselves and building their lives on the foundations of that mistake. But again, it must be remembered that the error is a part of human evolution."

"Then this must mean that multiplicities of ego, or the egoic aspect of all people, are basically different versions of the same thing: the negative pole of this polarity between ego and Spirit."

"Yes," she said. "Also, the combined thinking of every individual averages out as the vibration of global consciousness."

"It sounds as though most people are stuck in a faulty feedback-loop system involving the law of attraction, where, because of a displaced sense of identity, they attract a displaced picture of reality."

"In a way you are correct, but the laws of the universe aren't faulty. The problem is that most people experience only a projection of life through the transference of thought. They have unconsciously set mental blockages in place by assigning to limitations about their identity that directly color their perception of reality. This is the basis for what you might call *miscreating*."

Many of the concepts Gloria described came to me allegorically. I thought of myself as a camera in a movie theater. My thoughts about everything, including my beliefs about myself, was the film in front of the lens. The lamp that made the thoughtforms on the film visible on the screen of life was the light of life behind everything. The light was seen as neutral. I remained still and receptive as she moved forward with my enlightenment.

"It's important to understand how we function as universal beings—parts of a Greater Whole—rather than independent bodies with separate realities, which is what many of us dream to be. Such aspirations unknowingly limit our sense of identity, but it doesn't mean that any of us is good or bad. It simply means that we don't know what we're doing."

I thought about that and I couldn't get past the idea that what Gloria had just described sounded like a form of insanity.

"There is mental backwardness on a global scale. Many souls unknowingly allowed themselves to be overcome by their own mental projections to the point of defining themselves by them. This *is* insane. Such delusion automatically tries to protect itself, because its false reality has been set in the substance of Absolute Reality, *which is the backdrop of everything*, and is The Universal Intelligence from which we are extended. Due to this contrast, the error of identifying with the part of the mind that has split-off comes with a built-in sense of threat. As an unconscious defense against its unavoidable sense of inferiority, that disconnected, fragment of mind called ego inflates itself with a belief in its superiority, which manifests as every ugly act between individuals, and which mounts to conflicts among nations."

"On the surface, it appears that there are innumerable conflicts on earth, but you're saying that there is really only one conflict."

"Yes. That is correct. However, you must remember that everything I'm showing you illustrates *levels of consciousness*, which is what spirituality is all about. Mainstream religion doesn't know that the scriptures are a metaphorical externalization of states of human consciousness. It doesn't understand that Lucifer, Satan, Jesus, and every character in the Bible, aren't separate beings of form, but personified externalizations of every state of consciousness since the Creation, from which we are meant to learn. In other words—they are us!"

Gloria leaned toward me with a no-nonsense demeanor during this revelation, and all I could do was sit there, dumbfounded.

"At some point, humanity will have learned through their

suffering. They will cease identifying with an egoic splinter of mind, individually and collectively. People will become still in new knowledge, and when humanity reaches a critical mass of awakening, the Christ within will resurrect—as represented by the ascension of Jesus—to the reality that we are all part of One Universal Intelligence. In the most sacred of marriages, the relinquished ego will merge with divinity, and all souls will become Emmanuel—or *God-Men*. This is the long-awaited event in the history of the human species. "

Not only was I enthralled by the significance of what Gloria just said, but also at her glimmering aura, as she stood with her hands reaching up towards the heavens. "God-Men, Gloria? What will life be like then? I mean... what will we do? Are you a God-Woman?" I was eager to know since she had already performed a number of miraculous deeds, including gracing me with her presence.

Instead of a verbal response, she bowed and chuckled lightly —leaving me to wonder. "What you will do is create in extraordinary ways, Salvatore. God-Men are self-actualized and know how to manipulate the plasticity of the universe. This expression of your evolution will come when you are ready. You'll know more then. For now, just read about the history of the Masters, and examine the way they thought, spoke, and acted."

I had a persistent need to review much of what Gloria presented. It seemed to be a never-ending process of getting it, and then not getting it. But when I did get it, I understood more of it than I did before. So, I moved forward with my queries. "I feel uncomfortable with some of the things you say, Gloria. I mean... on one hand, what I'm hearing soothes me, like when you talk about Omnipresence. But when you speak of the ego, I feel like I'm not who I'm supposed to be, or something like that. Can't we just enjoy our ego personalities? They must have meaning, or why would we develop them?"

"Salvatore, you are feeling birth pangs in the classroom of life. You will always be who you are. It's your perception of yourself that's changing through a reinterpretation of the ego-self you made. Also, it is important to realize that there's a big difference between acknowledging your perception of life, and defining yourself by your perceptions, since as soon as you do the latter, you submit to limitation and become prideful, like Lucifer, by believing yourself to be the movie. This is the state where people begin to take themselves, or better said, what they believe to be themselves, way too seriously.

"What is referred to as *ego* isn't always *bad*. Enjoy your view of life, but it is of utmost importance that you stay grounded in reality by remembering that you color everything you see, and that you have the ability to change your movie, rather than allowing the movie that you made to rule over you."

Her words awakened me to a familiar stream of wordless thoughts that offered ideas concerning the placement of value. The thoughts gelled into the realization that we only value what we believe to be real.

"Thoughts of Omnipresence soothe you because the idea disentangles the illusion of separation while simultaneously teaching reverence for others," she said. "But it also turns the scope on your self-perceived identity. And, yes, that can be uncomfortable, even alarming, since that sense of identity presently anchors you."

"By saying that my identity anchors me, I'm assuming you mean my day-to-day familiarity with certain ways of viewing things, especially myself."

"Yes. Generally speaking, that limited sense of identity in everyone is fearful, and holds to thoughts of perfect safety by remaining unchangeable in a universe of motion. But that's the formula for resistance, which is the true cause of your anxieties. Rest assured, you won't be given more than you can handle. But trust me when I say that you are better off facing the fear of what you consider to be change. In facing the fear encountered during the reinterpretation of your beliefs about God and life, you will discover that you are truly changeless, over and above the limitation of any belief systems. You are asleep to life in thinking you have already made changes to the unchangeable. This is your mistake, your only sin."

This sounded quite deep to me. I wrestled with the idea of changelessness. I just kept asking myself, *Where is this part of me that is changeless?* "I hope what you're saying is that this growth is a step-by-step process, Gloria. I think humanity would prefer the kind of growth that happens through understanding, rather than by a forcing of views. Speaking of the truth, I am still somewhat resistant to changing my ideas about the way I see things, but I must admit that in the past, I was rewarded by every growth spurt I had initially resisted in my life."

"You will all grow at your own pace," she said in a solemn voice. "Some steps will seem harder than others, but your familiar way of living won't be torn from you. There will be things that fade from your interest, but you aren't going to lose anything. The more you learn, the better you will feel. In fact, you are better off living in the world according to the words of an old Gospel song: "This is the day that the Lord has made, let us rejoice and be glad in it…", and for the opportunity to learn from the lessons it offers," she added.

Gloria's reassurance soothed me. "I'm grateful that you've discussed some of your own pivotal points of learning," I said. "They've been immensely helpful in an overall sense. But what do you think would be most beneficial to me right now, at this particular stage of my development?"

She furrowed her brows and gazed at me intently for a few seconds. "Learn what it means to use your mind as a sense-tool. This is the lesson that will show you the ultimate definition of work. You are working toward remembering. Remembering who you are. You've defined yourself by your experiential movie, when *you are the light behind the film.* Your sense of identity is displaced—a detour taken by so many. You may serve a mistake for as long as it takes to learn the lesson of time, even into the afterlife; but until you release the past ideas you've allowed to define you, and return to your rightful place in the present moment, you will continue to lay marooned in fleeting, temporal experience, whether comfortably or uncomfortably."

"Did you say, *fleeting?*"

"Yes, I did, because nothing in the material world lasts. You aren't truly rooted in the temporal, psychological complexities of a limited identity. You may believe you are subjected to your own brand of justice in the reflections of your illusion, but remembering your home simply renders such mindsets meaningless. Even if it's dormant, you have within you the means to see from a much broader perspective."

I took a deep breath and rocked back and forth as I tried to digest what I was hearing. "Every time you talk like this, a whole new line of thought appears to change entire contexts of my thinking. I know I've held to past experiences, and I'm beginning to realize the extent to which I've defined myself by them. I just wonder how many I don't remember. I'm beginning to question how far back I have to look through my life experiences to find where I might have wrongly defined myself, and also set patterns. No sooner I think of one, another comes to take its place. It might sound strange to you, Gloria, but I don't know who I'd be without my false selves." Feeling winded, emotionally and physically, I took another deep breath and, with arms loosely folded across my chest, I lowered my head and leaned backwards.

"There only two sides to the coin of life: the reality of truth, which is the basis of love, and the delusion of the false, which gives rise to fear. What appears as many, is really but one false sense of self, Salvatore. But when the truth is known, every-thing false collapses. That's because the false has no real founda-tion. The point is that you are learning *what you are not,* from the angle of understanding. You are simply learning *to be.* It's a path. The one sin is that you fell asleep and lost sight of your true iden-tity as an extension of what you call God. The one solution is to wake up and remember the truth. Make movies that you can enjoy to the fullest. *That's what they're for.* But don't define yourself by any of them. That's pretty much what the metaphor of Adam and Eve, the snake, and eating from the tree of the knowledge of good and evil is all about."

14

A STATE OF GRACE FOREVER

"How people treat you is their karma; how you react is yours."

— Dr. Wayne Dyer

I recalled Gloria referring to Jesus as of the Christ Consciousness. I had a lot of questions about what his title meant, especially in regard to his stance on forgiveness. I always had trouble understanding why he would forgive the very ones who tortured and crucified him in such a horrific way, so I brought my concerns to her attention.

"Recall the words of Jesus as he suffered on the cross," she said. "'Father forgive them for they know not what they do.'"

"So, does this mean the people who crucified Jesus didn't know what they were doing because they'd lost sight of their core-identity? I'm trying to understand why, specifically, Jesus said to forgive them."

"Salvatore, that was a dark age when human perception was thoroughly distorted by minds so obscured by ignorance, people had no sense of the unity of Creation, at all. But Jesus attained

Christ Consciousness—the highest level of Mind. He volunteered to lead a great awakening to rekindle souls, to help them remember their original state and to cease reacting to the programs of the projecting egoic aspect of mind. Jesus was The Morning Star, The Way Shower, a Bringer of Light, who imparted knowledge to save the world from the hell projected by ignorance. Though not everyone understood his message as a light in the world, his consciousness *is* light, and it cannot help but bridge the perceived gap between the real and the unreal."

"But why did Jesus forgive his perpetrators? I would think they were in line for some kind of punishment before they were forgiven, at least."

Gloria looked at me and paused for some time. She turned slightly and lowered her head. I couldn't tell if she was mustering patience to deal with my oscillating states of mind, or if she was listening intently to someone.

"Listen closely," she finally said. "Since man's error about himself and about Creation is seen as a dissipating illusion from such a high state, punishment makes no sense in the frequency of forgiveness. People experience the energetic signature of whatever frequency they live in. In ways not so evident to you, all people are recompensed for everything that they think, say, and do. As an omniscient soul, Jesus knew this, simply because at the event of the involution of Creation, Jesus' soul did not disperse far from The Singularity from which all souls came. As a most highly attuned soul, he lowered his vibration to the density of the physical dimension to become the embodiment of Cosmic Consciousness. He often spoke of forgiveness, because his level of mind was, is, and always will be forgiveness, itself—the acknowledgment of what we all are, as *given* at the *fore* of Creation."

I felt somewhat perturbed that I, too, was interlaced with a dissipating illusion of life because I sensed that I must be on the wrong side of it all. I had to be, since I still struggled with the idea of forgiveness, especially in extreme cases.

The sister clarified without my even asking the question. "The idea of forgiveness arises automatically in your dimension because so many live in accordance to a mistake. Yet, Spirit is in a state of grace and is able to rise above, and all people, as spiritual entities, *are in a state of grace forever.* Those who have yet to see the meaning in Jesus' living words and the truth in other Masters of the same Mind, still lust after hope in false doctrines; subsequently, due to their distorted beliefs of sin and inequalities, they repeat the same error about identity."

Earlier, when Gloria had said that we have an energetic signature, I had taken that to mean we experience the emotion of our own mentality. For example, if I hated someone, I was the one feeling the hate, not the person I hated. The image of a hand pointing an accusatory finger with the other four fingers pointing back at the accuser came to mind, and Gloria's account of forgiveness began to make sense. I knew I'd be addressing forgiveness again, but just a few moments ago I was really thrown when she associated lust with hope. I decided or, should I say, dared, to open up the topic of sex and lust. "Gloria, you said that people lust after hope in false doctrines. I've always heard of lust only as it relates to sex, so are there other interpretations of lust?"

"The true definition of lust is unyielding attempts to find fulfillment in things that can never fulfill you. Satisfying sexual desires is not fulfillment, and lust isn't only about sex. Sex stands out because taboos concerning sexuality have been duplicated and reinforced throughout hundreds of generations."

I knew what a taboo was, but I wanted her to explain it in further detail, so I asked, "What is a taboo, Gloria, and how did this one begin?"

"When anything is prohibited for so-called sacred reasons, it's called taboo. Stemming from a misunderstanding of original sin, human sexuality has had a lid placed upon it. This causes resistance. Such resistance places suppressed sexuality in an explosive position, just like it would in any other blocked energetic flow."

"So, this taboo started with religion?"

"Yes, it did, which caused religion to be a breeding ground for negativity when addressing sexuality. This is why many people experience levels of sexual dysfunction throughout their lives. Some dysfunctions lead to sexual abuse, and, are largely a result of repressing an already distorted cultural sense of human nature. Since societies have a way of permeating themselves with ancient misconstrued ideas, blocking what is natural has repercussions, even for those who don't consider themselves religious. Powerful religious institutions and their offshoots are the cause. They have misinterpreted much, and, injected mental poison into the roots of civilization from which it has compounded."

Now that I had a better understanding about the origins and the meaning of taboo, I decided to ask the sister about one in particular that religious leaders and several governments around the globe fight passionately against. "In regard to inter-personal relationships, where do people who prefer same-sex unions stand on the Grand Cosmic Scale? There is much controversy about it, ranging from same-sex marriage, to acts of violence, and even murder. There are religions that believe same-sex attractions are a sin against God. Is this true?"

"Not in reality, my friend, but only in the limited thinking of those who still don't understand the definition of sin itself. To judge and condemn others is to perceive inequality, which *is* the problem—or sin—of the world that leads to every form of conflict. Those who classify certain groups as especially sinful are perpetuating the one sin of which they are still unaware."

"But I was told that God hates a variety of other people, too, such as drunkards and thieves. Why do people involved with religions persist in repeating this ideology?"

"Because they are projecting images onto the screen of life through their belief-ridden movies. Anyone who believes that God hates, neither has a real idea of God, nor do they understand the dynamic of mental projection. Through the mirroring of their own limited thoughts, they make an image of a *God* who possesses the traits of men, and then wish to destroy others in his name—all the while believing such a reversal of truth acts in favor of salvation. But salvation is beyond the thin layer of ordinary thinking; it's about coming out of conflict, *completely.* There is no partiality to salvation. Although some may think so, no one has ever found the pathway to truth while sitting on a throne of judgment—the unconscious defense mechanism they have unknowingly projected —one they think pleases God. People need to understand that it's a reversal of the truth to think that God is human-like, when in fact it's humans who are made in the image of God. The problem here is that most humans still don't know what they are as universal beings."

Everything she said made perfect sense, but I wanted to get a clearer picture. "Can you further explain why people think we are made in the image and likeness of God, yet still believe God acts like a man?"

"When people hear that we are made in the image of God, they think it means that *He* is in the form of a man and that he has the potential to be a jealous, and even hateful being. But people tend not to look beyond the world of form, so they miss the truth in those profound scriptural words. The purpose of the words was to help people see beyond their limited experiential perception of themselves, and to come out of their mental boxes. This is what spirituality is all about, and it's much more profound than forcing change to their behaviors. But instead, many continue to turn the most important truth around and take a backward point of view."

"I can see how this upside-down picture of God wrought

havoc in the world. When it comes to people being involved with anything having to do with God, everyone wants to be on the side they think is winning," I said.

Gloria gave me an affirming nod. "There is also no physical gender in spirit, Salvatore. Same-sex partners are subject to the same universal laws as any other human interactions. Ostracizing and attacking others for any reason, including sexual orientation, reflects the inner conflict behind the eyes of the viewer. To use a personal concept of God as a reason to harm others is a sure sign of allegiance to a desperately derelict ego, attempting to save itself by constantly replenishing its energy with the accolades of some form of group-think. The truth is that each of you was created both male and female, which isn't specifically about physical gender or sexuality, nor about cultural roles as men and women, but about directing creative energy. When appraising spiritually, which as a spiritual being you must learn to do, it is understood that the infusion of an idea and the womb of manifestation of that idea are the respective masculine and feminine aspects within each complete person. Men, women, and procreation are but an outer expression of these two inner poles of creating. For this to make sense, you must elevate your sight and open yourself to the knowledge that, above all, we are divine creators beyond the phys-ical—not mere men and women.

"On a different level," she continued without hesitation, "as part of their evolution, souls must experience incarnating into both sexes. So, after being one gender for a number of lifetimes, when a soul incarnates as the opposite gender, it may carry with it a residual frequency of the gender of its previous incarnations. This manifests in degrees across a spectrum in the physical world. It is not wrong or bad. It is natural. Another reason why such highly evolved souls choose such an arduous task as they enter this world, is to bring people face-to-face with their judgment with the hope that they will transcend it, as we all must. When it comes to intimate relationships, gender preference doesn't matter. *What is important, is that you love.*"

As I listened intently to Gloria's earnest revelations, I recalled the few times in my life when I thought I had truly loved someone, whether male or female. There was no feeling like it. I had read that love is unselfish, so I wondered if what I felt was love, since I loved with the desire to be loved in return.

Afraid I might not like her answer, I asked my next question rather tentatively. "Gloria, I've been pondering on thoughts of love, and there have been times when I've wondered if it's selfish to want to be loved in return when you deeply love someone."

"You can relax about my answer, Salvatore," she said, with a discerning smile. "The desire to be loved in return is as natural as the rising and setting of the sun and the moon. However, when your need becomes obsessive, the pain it causes signals a sense of incompleteness in you. But when you love from the fullness of your true identity, there is no sense of neediness, because there is no fear of loss. You have to be in the correct consciousness to share love, and when you are, you're able to feel the love much more."

Gloria spoke very ardently about this topic, I thought—probably because she wanted me to avoid more of what had already caused pain in my life. "Loving someone from a sense of the incompleteness you mentioned has been the cause of terrible emotional pain in my life. I never want to go through it again," I assured her.

"In matters like this, the learning is in the doing," she said, with a look of sadness. "But you will learn," she added, as her lips curled into a soft smile.

Gloria stood and interlaced her fingers above her solar plexus and instructed me to do the same. She explained that this was a position used for the acceptance of healing energy, and then she proceeded to make an invocation:

"May the Sublime Essence of the Cosmic infuse our beings and cleanse us of all impurities of mind and body, so that we may become channels through which the universal forces may heal and alleviate pain. So may it be."

We remained standing for about three minutes, after which time she motioned for me to sit with her again. I felt as renewed as Gloria looked. Then she proceeded to speak.

"Salvatore, when I refer to sexuality as a natural part of being human, I'm not condoning promiscuity, promoting irresponsibility, nor am I condemning anyone involved in such behavior. What I'm addressing are the guilt-producing beliefs, regarding sexuality itself, as being inherently wrong. Beliefs are thoughts, and thought-forms are energy. Such insidious beliefs cause an energetic imbalance by instilling resistance to a natural human attribute. This makes for a pressure-cooker-effect, which results in extremes of behavior. In accordance with natural law, *what we resist persists*—and consequently produces more guilt. Despite the fact that it's *false* guilt based on internalizing erroneous belief systems; it still causes shame—the most detrimental emotional energy pertaining to one's sense of self-worth. When shame-based resistance blocks energetic flow, energetic forces can mount like rising water against a dam. Look closely at the unit of your physical, mental, and emotional body, and you will see electromagnetism behaving under those same laws, with some form of mental-emotional resistance at the root of most disease."

"How does all this affect the way people in such belief systems feel?" I asked. "Can they feel good about themselves?"

"Sometimes people have to learn, not only to feel good about themselves, but they also need to understand what it means to love themselves, and that happens through growth. True self-love develops when you *know*, that above and beyond any experiences in your life, you're forever an extension of divinity. It's the key to self-acceptance in every area of your life that is required to move you out of resistance, *through and beyond* who and what you think you are as a being."

Gloria looked squarely at me while speaking her last truths. I had the distinct feeling that even though her statement was universal, she was directing it particularly at me. I became so uncomfortable, I immediately changed the subject—probably because I couldn't recall ever having any thoughts about loving myself, or even thinking that I was supposed to. "When people get lost in focusing on external things, such as painful relationships, and can't seem to change their experience of the world around them for the better, what can they do to help themselves?"

"Before any desired outer change is accomplished, you must know that externals don't change of themselves, because they are *effects*. In order to change what is seen *outside*, one must first consider the Law of Cause and Effect, and go *inside* to find the cause. When the cause is found to be part of a chain of effects made by a cultural collective of mundane ideas, then the seeker has opened his or her mind enough to look beyond effects and toward First Cause. This is the way to Self-Actualization. But before you can go within and allow for any real change to happen, you must first acknowledge, and, fully accept your perception of yourself exactly the way you are, right there on the surface of your mind. That's where self-love comes in, Salvatore."

I felt lassoed back to the topic of self-love. It led me to believe that above all else, she thought I needed this information. I pitched another probing question. "Why don't more people look into the mirror of self?"

"Many people are prevented from looking within and taking this often difficult, yet, required step on the pathway of truth because they remain controlled by fear and guilt. Keep your account short in this respect. The longer you run from the necessity of turning inward to face yourself, the further you will stray into insanity, and the harder your inevitable depolarization will be."

"Information like this still has a way of making me feel uncomfortable," I admitted. "All that talk about changing identity scares me, and almost makes me feel like I'm losing myself. Could I go insane, Gloria?"

"You are insane already, but only to a degree like most of the world," she said, in a casually calm and relaxed tone. "You may feel like you're losing yourself, but that's because somewhere in your mind, you sense you have already abandoned yourself. At a magnitude of time you cannot comprehend, your first experience of change was when you forgot your relationship to Creation—the only real thing about you. This is why changing your perception of yourself now, frightens you into thinking you are losing something. Thought, along those lines, is delusional. You may perceive, through *your eyes,* that you are losing something, but through the eyes of Absolute Reality, you can never lose anything," she concluded, raising her hands in the surrender position on the heel of her last words.

When Gloria said that we can never truly lose anything, I came to realize that she was speaking from the level of soul, which is in the realm of eternal sensing. "Your mistaken ego echoes abandonment," she interjected my thoughts, "but only because the ego senses that you're ascending to a broader perspective and that you are beginning to realize that it isn't you. You're now learning how to realign your sight to understanding the meaning behind The Golden Rule of Life. This realignment is far removed from your past reactions to ego-formulated and religious sin-concepts with their false guilt and punishment. Soon, you'll know freedom as your most precious attribute."

Gloria grew quiet, and in the ensuing silence, I thought about Jack, and how it seemed impossible to share concepts with him that didn't align with his interpretation of every word in the Bible.

The greatest irony was that I actually did see all this truth in the Scriptures. The paradox of how two or more people could look at the same thing and see it so differently, brought home the meaning of perspective.

After her short break, Gloria was ready to move forward with my spiritual training. "No matter how many times or in how many ways religions preach it, there is no God waiting to punish you, Salvatore. Misguided people punish themselves. Remember, you never have vision through other's eyes when it comes to knowing your own identity as a universal being. You are free to take in the belief of others, but for whatever reason you choose to do so, know that it's from that decision you paint your world. You are truly awakening when you begin to realize you have stenciled your sight in this way."

"If all of what you say about evolution and awakening is the way out of the perceived world, then what is taking so long for the lesson to be learned?" I asked, with restrained impatience.

"Error makes for a hardness of heart that's based in fear. But it cannot last. The world you know, including many of its religions, is poisoned by limited thinking. But I tell you, the truth about life is more powerful than lies. A realignment is happening, and it will shine away ignorance in the waking of all people," Gloria said with emphasis, as though she were relieved to have imparted that particular message.

"Will science eventually merge with spirituality and bring such saving news to the world?" I asked.

"The truth about Creation waits to be discovered within each person. While science stands in the temple of truth, spirituality and scientific theory are generally opposed in the world. When man believes scientific theories about his place in the universe, knowledge of scientific facts is delayed to the detriment of the human race. Jesus, and other Masters, knew the truth about Self. Using their mastery over the science of being, they applied the highest laws of nature to perform what were called miracles. Most scientists of your day are entangled in repetitious theory, and they bring the masses along with them, when humanity would be better served if it learned what the ancient mystics knew."

"Well, I won't say that I can't relate to resisting change. But considering the mess the world is in right now, we are surely in desperate need of it." I felt my patience waning, not with Gloria, but with the state of the world and the beliefs of those we place in charge.

"The world appears daunting, but don't let that stop you from doing your small part. At some point in time, you will see how every kindness and every awakening to truth lift the whole," she said, with a triumphant-like wave of her hands.

"So, each person's thoughts have an effect on the collective consciousness of the entire planet?" I queried further.

"Oh, yes, Salvatore! But people have a tendency to resist change, despite evidence that the present paradigm could lead to their own destruction. In the past, scientists and theologians alike experienced great upheaval when it was discovered that Earth was not the center of the universe. Old beliefs, especially those of the past millennium, aren't relinquished easily by most, even when the fallacy of those beliefs becomes evident. But there always comes a time in mediocrity when people are ready to grow away from the false sense of security found in the familiar, a time when they recognize the old way of thinking as a springboard to higher learning."

15

THE RECOGNITION OF POWER

"As far as ignorance is concerned, not just Buddhism, but every religion recognizes it as the source of suffering."

— The 14th Dalai Lama

Satisfied with the sister's explanation about the world's reluctant attitude to change, I still wanted to pursue more discussion about illusory identities, their reactive behavior, and their causes. These subject matters had triggered a sense of dread in me. "I realize this is a little off topic, Gloria, but why would God allow any kind of mistake to happen in the first place, particularly one having to do with our core-identity?"

"Salvatore, it would serve you well to contemplate what is presented to you a little more closely. You keep going back to your old system of thought, when in reality, there is no God sitting on a throne somewhere making allowances for things, like kings, queens, and dictators do. To forget this fact, and instead align with the beliefs of those who think there is such a God, makes for a sense of vulnerability, and, as a result, fear is generated—which reflects the error of your mental state.

"From a larger perspective, fear is a sign that much power has been placed in too small a space. Fear is the walls of the space under pressure, and that space is a mindset. The walls are proof that humans, who are created from All Power, have defined themselves by something much smaller than what they truly are: the limited beliefs of an insufficient psychology. Those who have locked themselves into this sort of mistake, fear the fear—the walls laced with their belief systems—feeling that without them they would be utterly lost. When those walls are threatened, the fear can become so intense that their architects gravitate toward the center of their self-made prisons, and exclusion becomes the mainstay of defense for the stronghold they've made."

"What, exactly, do you mean by they become exclusive in order to defend themselves and, who, or, what, are these architects?"

"I'm referring to groups of people, such as the followers of some religions, who draw from a delusion of righteousness found in the *power of agreement* among themselves. They prey ruthlessly on others whom they judge as unrighteous. They attempt to fill their emptiness with a sense of superiority by behaving like energy vampires. Yet, the thirst that drives them can only be quenched by a truth they don't see. They ride the momentum of their investment in the false, and tenaciously adhere to their beliefs, while inflating themselves in the arrogance of thinking that they could actually offend, what they believe to be God."

Gloria stopped talking, and once again stood up, and suggested that I join her in reverence to the singularity in all things. Once on my feet, she instructed me to be still. And in that moment of stillness, I acknowledged a stream of white light pouring in from the cosmic. It entered me through the top of my head, coursed downward through my body, and exited through my feet into the ground. The experience was breathtaking, to say the least.

"This cleansing exercise is known as a *light flush*," she said smiling at me. "I felt as though you needed it. But before we resume, let's take three, long, deep breaths together."

As we synchronized our deep breathing, I felt much more focused and receptive as if the light and the energy from our breaths had unplugged previously clogged areas of my being.

"Now you're ready," Gloria said, and indicated with her hand that we retake our seats.

I *was* ready, and anxious to resume our discussion. "Can you tell me more about what you called energy vampires? Are there actually people who feed off the energy of others?"

"Yes, there are. When you, as an electromagnetic being of energy, are unaware of your cosmic essence, you are distracted from receiving your full measure of cosmic energy, your high frequency protection, and your life sustenance. When you don't fill yourself with the truth of your own being, your frequency is lowered, and you become vulnerable in this state. You become as food for the lower thought-forms of others living in both the physical and non-physical dimensions. Like bees to honey, they attract and attach to the like-vibration of your auric field.

"These thought-forms have been called *demons*, but like everything else in the universe, they are but frequencies. The malicious egos that generate lower thoughts have a need to defend their encapsulated identities. To do so, they use what is perceived as fault in others, in an attempt to prove their own righteousness, while simultaneously ensuring good-standing among their group-think. The sense of empowerment these types of egos feel is temporary. Anyone who's so blind to the All-Inclusiveness of Spirit will continue to sense lack in some way, and the idiopathic feeling that something is missing will always pose a threat."

Keeping in line with all of her theories, this one was right on point. "I've never thought of such concepts in this way," I said. "You sure add another dimension to the bullies of the world."

"Unfortunately, dark mindsets blanket much of the world. They come in groups of organized egos that have formed suppressive systems, such as religions. These groups manipulate people mentally, physically, and emotionally. As members of these organizations walk in the belief of their own psychoses, they wield guilt, fear, and shame, which act as temporary fixes to give them control and replenish their sense of superiority. But their targets are only susceptible to such manipulations when, they, too, are unaware of their own connection to the universe."

"With so many people unaware of the truth you teach, it's no wonder there's so much strife in every area of life." I shook my head in sorrow for my fellow humans.

"I agree, but the truth will come to pass. In a world marred by all manner of violence, including war, suicide, and students exploding in classrooms and killing their peers—along with other incomprehensible acts of murder and genocide—it's imperative that people learn to be still, and examine the roots of identity. There is a great need to uncover the dynamics at work beneath the insanity in everyday life. Be grateful for teachers of the fundamentals of thought—particularly those who enlighten others to the synchronicity of identity, belief, and perception—for they are bringing light to the world."

"I believe my mystical mentors are among these teachers. They continue to show me how to see life in a better way."

"Yes, they are. The true teachers are the ones who know the perceivable world doesn't just happen externally. They explain the science of manifesting, and how the world is influenced by the intent of everyone as co-creators in a moldable, energetic realm. Many are coming to understand the principles of the mental universe as they apply to perception. People are shown how they perceive through mental lenses colored by mixtures of beliefs inculcated by religion, culture, life experiences, and their interpretations of those beliefs."

"Can you give me other examples of how our beliefs create our perception of reality? I always find the idea fascinating."

"Wear a filter of blue-tinted eyeglasses, and see blue; wear red, and see red. The colored glasses can never be your identity, Salvatore. Knowing that our thoughts act in much the same way to create our perception of reality is to hold the key of life, and the wisdom we acquire reveals how correcting the lens of our minds promotes clarity. Its gift is a dispensation of the grace that was there in principle, all along, yet appreciated only through the art of true observation. Don't you know that this is what you are learning, Salvatore?"

"Yes— I do. I'm just not accustomed to the thought that I will eventually become a light in the world."

Gloria looked at me with her head slightly tilted, eyes fully open, and a knowing smile filled with promises of imminent surprises. "Salvatore, you've been shown that the natural state of all existence is unified at a level over and above any beliefs. The population's lens on life is clouded because people have *too much* belief, even to the point of obscuring the universal truth that what we call God, our Source, is the Light that's in all people."

I knew that the light the sister mentioned was much more than what I had experienced when she performed the *light flush* on me a few minutes ago. "I keep hearing about this light within," I said, "but I've yet to see it. When I close my eyes, there is only darkness."

"Be patient. It is true that in order to grow one must look within for the light beyond the superficial mind, but this isn't a glaring physical light as seen by the human eye. The light I speak of is gentle, and not perceived through the organic senses. Yet, this light is everywhere, in everything, and when you see it, you will know it. Though you don't fully comprehend this now, the light will reveal forgiveness as an automatic process."

"How?"

"Through acts of forgiveness, you cast away grievances that held you in the smallness of the world you think you made. As the sacred seed in you flourishes with the fertilization of forgiveness, your consciousness will expand, attuning you to higher levels of receptivity and vision. Your heightened perception will lead you to a complete re-identification of your being. Such transformation awaits all of humanity."

"I think I'm beginning to understand forgiveness with a new sense," I murmured. "I see it in the same way that I think I perceive the light."

"And what way is that?" the sister asked.

"As an all-permeating vastness."

She nodded her head. "You are beginning to understand the meaning of Oneness. Flow with the freedom you find in the light with the knowledge that we create our own perception of reality. To understand and respond to this truth is to accept your part in the great awakening."

"Thank you, Gloria. I actually get that! This is all so profound." However, I still had a subtle sense of uneasiness that never seemed to completely go away.

"Yes, it is infinitely profound, and worth every discomfort you feel in the depolarization of insufficient, hand-me-down beliefs. When greater truth and flashes of insight light the edges of your consciousness, the dynamics at work behind the streaming scenes of life will be exposed, and you will see that there could never be a gap between truth and what does not exist."

"When I look at the suffering of the world, I sometimes wonder if our prayers are heard at all. I still don't understand why there is so much pain, especially when it comes to children." This issue was something that bothered me deeply.

"Atrocities that occur on earth do give the appearance that prayers aren't answered, and that there is no God who would allow for such suffering. But to be still and know God, is to realize that as beings created from Omnipotence in a universe of neutrality, humans have the attribute of power, and the free will to choose how to direct that power to manifest thought into form and action. The basis for *misdirecting* the power of thought lies in the great misperception humankind has of its identity as being separated. In contrast to the reality of our unity, the power is directed into reacting to the idea of conflicting differences. Through its own momentum, a grid of thought-energy stemming from this original mistake encompasses the world. The mistake has been compounding and weaving a network ever since the beginning of time, or the involution. It's the cause of all misery and actually the reason for the perception of time itself."

Since I felt so passionate about this particular topic, I gave myself completely over to the sound of Gloria's voice and allowed her words, that seemed to have a life of their own, to penetrate to the very core of my being.

"Due to the belief in separation, your minds, bodies, and emotions—as a unit—have been constantly exposed to unfavorable energetic patterns for countless generations, even to affecting the structure of human DNA. But do not fear this. Although the process has built upon itself since time immemorial, one single awakening to Omniscience is enough to disintegrate a multitude of error. You need only to practice identification with the truth— an act, not embroiled in religious debate, but which is about recognizing what Jesus, Paramahansa Yogananda, and other enlightened souls came to share throughout the ages."

Transformation was the name of the game these days. My thoughts about reality increased, and the more they did, the more I experienced a sound, in, and around me. "I often hear a sound, Gloria, a faint hum in the air that I associate to something awakening within me. I get the feeling that the light we're talking about, and this sound, are one and the same."

Gloria looked away and seemed thoughtful for a moment. When she met my gaze again, her face had a softer glow to it. "They are the same, but at complementary frequencies that infuse you with healing. You are hearing the *Hum of the Universe* from the foundation of life. A series of ups and downs may throw you off kilter, but you will always return to walk in the light of truth. The sound and the light are the Two Principles underlying all of Creation, and they are there to remind you that you are never alone."

16

KNOWING WHAT YOU ARE NOT

"Too often we underestimate the power of a touch, a smile, a kind word, a listening ear, an honest compliment, or the smallest act of caring, all of which have the potential to turn a life around."

— Leo Bascaglia

Every time Gloria spoke about perceiving from a falsely based sense of identity, it increasingly hit home. When one denies his or her being as part of something greater, how could there not be a naturally coinciding sense of lack even at an unconscious level, since it involved all the power of the universe. It would be tantamount to one color of a rainbow denying that it, and the other colors, all came from white light.

Gloria's voice cut into my musings. "When we act from temporal ideas based in separation, the blind choices we make commence a domino effect and attract still lower thought-vibration that leads to realms of greater obscurity. Someone walking a sleeping path can become so distanced from knowledge of their very being as part of The All, that they develop a growing sense of alienation; then through the projecting mechanism of mind, they alienate others and commit the kinds of heinous acts that cross the limits of ordinary human understanding."

"But how does that happen, Gloria? Why would anyone think in such a way?"

"They don't know who they are, or why they act the way they do in the neutrality of the Law, or even that there are Universal-Natural Laws. In such a state, the unaware mind duplicates itself onto other people and onto the screen of the world, then ultimately wages attacks on its own projections. The projections are perceived as separate and external, when they're actually the intolerable parts of *that* mind cast outward in dissociation. One could even come to see murder as a form of displaced suicide."

I dared to voice my fears. "What you're describing is disturbing, Gloria. It actually sounds as if we're confusing real life with a bad movie."

A look of surprise appeared on Gloria's face. "Salvatore, these things aren't new. I'm describing everyday occurrences. Life becomes equivalent to a bad movie when uncorrected belief intensifies the emotions. With no mental ventilation in place, people who believe in their own alienation feel severely threatened. Early in their lives, they became victims of the degrading thoughts of others; they mistakenly accepted these thoughts as their own, and then compounded them into nightmares."

"It's a frightening thought to be completely in the dark to the point of feeling alienated."

"No person can be completely without light, yet there are blind souls who give momentum to the original error which you already know as the lie passed down through the generations. They have no concept of real giving. Instead of giving to receive, they take, yet they achieve no real gain. Even self-medicating addicts, who've passed on without awakening, may still seek relief by attaching their energetic body to the energy field of like-minded physical counterparts. As discarnate energy, they siphon from people of like-vibration who are living in the physical world. Like attracts like, and regardless of the mindset, it's always a matter of frequency."

"How scary. I used to drink a lot and it makes me wonder if there were times when I had companions!"

"Yes, you did, and there were times when you couldn't stop because you were drinking for three."

"Please tell me you're joking," I said with a mixture of fear and passive recognition of the truth in her words.

"I wouldn't joke about such things. The truth is that, some of the bars you visited had more discarnate souls, than they did flesh and blood patrons. The Law of Attraction is constant, so be grateful for your humility and for the courage to face, accept, and learn to know yourself, or, *what you are not.*"

I cringed at the thought of discarnate souls feeding off me. "Given the magnitude of the various outcomes, one would think the people of the world would know these things by now, Gloria."

"Seek and ye shall find. Knock and the door to truth will be opened to you. To create frequencies that attract what is sought, people must fervently ask from a place deep within themselves. The Bible, and other inspirations, have referred to this process for centuries. Yet, clarity about the workings of identity, belief, and perception, or what is real and what is not, still isn't sermonized, not even from the pulpits of many churches. As Jesus of the Christ Consciousness said, "Let he who has ears to hear…""

"Can I take this to mean that I'm walking the right path now, and that I don't have to worry about attracting lower vibrations?" I asked.

"Your path is *your* path; it was never wrong. How else would you have learned? Just remember the laws, and that your dark night of the soul has long passed."

"At times, it seems as if you're saying that it's bad to have a belief system. I mean, don't we have to believe in something?" I probed.

"There is no judgment of good or bad here. From my standpoint, I am able to discern the difference between mental freedom and imprisonment in the physical realm. Most people in your dimension don't see that difference. Not all belief is erroneous. *I only want you to understand the dynamics of belief.*"

"I understand that our beliefs create the reality we see. Can you elaborate on that? I'd like to see it from a variety of angles."

"Yes, of course. The subject of belief could always use some dilation," she said, on a deep breath. "The mental images you cast onto the screen of the world are formed from the thoughts and beliefs you hold. Losing conscious governance over your own creative imagination can cause nightmares in your life; these nightmares appear as external to you because you're unaware that they are the reflected images of the thoughts you hold within."

"So then, belief can work for us, or against us?"

"It most certainly can, Salvatore. You are designed to consciously create your own reality through imagery, yet much of humanity blindly use the law of creation in reverse by allowing their imagery to control them. You are free to effectuate the latter, but since you're an extension of Infinite Wisdom, you wouldn't consciously choose to do so. Your purpose does not involve imprisonment by images rooted in anyone else's thought systems, religious or otherwise."

I started to wonder if Gloria knew me better than I knew myself. I carefully listened with a growing sense of hunger for knowledge about my own self-perception in relation to the way others perceive me.

"You have the power to hurt yourself through a misstep you made in the dark, but your power grows exponentially once you gain the ability to see what you're doing. People who are stuck in fearful mind-constructs tend to cling to what they identify with, and as a result, they remain blind to their own freedom, and continue to make pictures inside, while thinking they come from outside.

"The truth, Salvatore, is that you're immeasurably lifted in choosing to overlook their mistakes. See them from beyond their beliefs to the core of their being—even if necessarily from a distance. This is *high frequency living.* If they are opened to learning, you must use all available opportunities to show them what you see; this is also how you learn. The meaning of giving to receive becomes evident in this act."

The meaning of giving to receive in this way escaped me. I sifted through my mind for a connection but since I couldn't find one, I concluded that I failed to perceive her intended meaning. "Can you be clearer on how overlooking error is giving to receive?" I asked.

"I would love to! Have you ever heard of the word, *namaste?*"

"Yes. I've heard the word many times. Isn't it a Hindu greeting?"

"More than a simple greeting, it's an act that symbolizes supreme reverence. When you bow to anyone with your palms together at your face or chest, and say the salutation, *namaste,* you're actually saying: *from the divinity in me, to the divinity in you…*"

"What a beautiful definition!" I exclaimed, deeply moved.

"The salutation overlooks everything in a person, except their innate divinity. It's a simultaneous recognition of the holiness in ourselves and also in others. Can you see how this is an act of giving, while receiving at the same time?" she asked.

"Well, yes! I can, Gloria," I said in astonished recognition as a sense of singularity washed over me like a wave.

"Salvatore, what we're talking about is the same as forgiveness. People commonly think that *sins* are forgiven, but that's incorrect. Sins—as we call them—are overlooked, not forgiven."

The expression on Gloria's face made it seem like she

expected I would ask a lot more questions about sin and the meaning of forgiveness. She was right. "This could only mean that forgiveness is about giving and receiving. Is that right?"

"Exactly. Forgiveness is the state of mind that overlooks error while acknowledging the soul. It stems from higher, fifth dimensional thinking, and it's where conflicts become doorways leading out of, and, beyond self-made mental prisons."

"I must confess that your semantical depictions aren't always easy for me to follow, Gloria, but they certainly energize my thinking. Could you talk more on the subject of forgiveness then?"

"We'll talk more about forgiveness later, my friend. You've had enough for now. These things take time to percolate," she said, while slowly gliding her hands in a downward direction over her forearms, just as she had done several times before.

She'd explained that these movements were to keep her frequency high, so I waited until she returned her attention to me before I asked my next question. "Gloria, your teaching portrays freedom amid entanglements. Will people ever understand the truth, and stop relentlessly associating God with fear?"

"As surely as the sun rises, it will come to pass. There is nothing simpler than the truth, Salvatore. Only the false is complex. Each soul who realizes the truth, raises the vibration of all creation. Remember this: when you witness a higher perspective dissolving the false mental clutter of the world, you are nearing the day, when in a flash, you will be changed into something beyond anything you've ever dreamed."

I had once questioned the difference between mental transformation and *metamorphosis*. I thought they could never be the same. Metamorphosis involved physicality, so did it mean we would change physically at a point in our evolution? Since I knew Gloria had all the answers to my questions, I asked, "Are transformation and metamorphosis different degrees of the same process?"

"Stop to think about what is meant by Oneness," she said,

raising a finger. "Everything is part of everything else. Nothing is excluded. So, of course this means that the mind and body are a unit, thus, when mentality changes, the body also changes."

At that moment, I became aware that I held unconscious limitations around the idea of Oneness, which meant that I hadn't fully grasped the concept, even though Gloria had spoken about it earlier. Her next statement alerted me to the fact that she'd read my mind.

"At the level of change concerning genuine spiritual transformation, even DNA is affected by the higher frequencies of thought-energy, Salvatore. Ascending levels of consciousness nourish the physical-spiritual substance of a gateway within; this process leads to the physical change, and the higher octaves of receptivity you are coming to know."

Even though Gloria had already imparted related knowledge on the subject, every new angle she addressed continued to challenge and expand my thinking. I felt the meaning behind her words, and even her thoughts, if that were possible. They lifted me. My whole being tasted them for what they were: the nectar of truth.

As I grappled with the insights, she looked at me lovingly, and said, "Vision may be dim for a while longer, Salvatore, and there may be times when you feel incomplete and subjected to every manner of suffering, but don't you worry. The illusions in which humanity has been looping sit like feathers before the winds of eternity. Trust that there will come a time when they will blow away from your sight in a rush of absolute joyfulness."

17

THE SELF-SEPARATED MIND

"Being on a spiritual path does not prevent you from facing times of darkness. But it teaches you how to use the darkness as a tool to grow."

— Unknown

I took Gloria's last words to mean that the ways of history would one day disappear. How could this not be the case, since everything humanity had based life on would melt away with the integration of a higher truth? But when would this happen? I wanted a closer look at what was preventing an age of enlightenment from blanketing the world. "This all sounds so earth-moving, Gloria. However, I wish I could understand why this change is taking so long to come about."

"It revolves around fear, Salvatore, and you're nearing the time when you'll have first-hand experience of what that means."

Although I heard what she said, it did not immediately register in my mind, and instead of asking her to explain exactly what she meant, I just stood there, eagerly receptive to the rest of her answer.

"Since people have a way of holding tightly to the residuals of ancient paradigms, the dead fruit of belief associated to a distant past colors the reality of the unwitting. As in the case of many throughout history, fear associated with a concept of God, is always due to the mental weaving of deluded mindsets. As you know, there is a marked similarity between the way a camera projects images onto a movie screen, and the way people make images of their own ideas of God from misinterpreted teachings of the past. But people aren't inanimate cameras; they have within themselves the ability to discern whether or not to internalize the thoughts of others. What truly, free person would accept ideas leading to a nightmare ruled by a wrathful God?" Gloria asked with pursed lips.

From past experiences and relationships, I knew exactly what she was talking about. There were many people I knew who were afraid of the image they held of God: as a man with every worst human trait. They had real concerns that they might not live up to God's expectations, and that they would go to hell to burn forever and ever.

"God is love, and far beyond the love that the world knows," Gloria stated with a sparkle of knowledge and reverence in her eyes. "Those who claim freedom by preaching otherwise have no idea who Jesus was, or why his message was about forgiveness."

"So, what you're saying is that there are a lot of people claiming to be free, when they're not, yet think that they are?" I asked with a confused look.

"Yes. But in truth, all souls are perpetually free. It's only when they cloak themselves under a web of bondage to untruths, that they become blind to their freedom and power. Much of humanity is deluded in such occurrences that stem from a mistaken interpretation of the sin-concept. This delusion becomes evident when people parrot scripture while teaching that the Creator doesn't know sin, yet, they, themselves, still condemn others. Therein lays proof of an unyielding belief in the underpinnings of a self-separated mind.

"The self-separated mind is a pain-producing illusion," she continued with intent emphasis. "That inner fortress, laced with the belief in many sins, death, lack, fear, guilt, and shame, is but a blind perspective, haunted by undertones concerning the possibility of abandonment by God."

The momentum in Gloria's voice slowed and her tone softened in what appeared to be sadness as she neared the end of her last statement.

In an attempt to lift her mood, I said, "I understand how this happens through internalizing the beliefs of others, Gloria."

"Do you really, Salvatore?" she asked, dubiously.

"I think so," I replied with reserve to her apparent skepticism. For the most part, I understood her explanations, but I kept experiencing lapses. There were moments when my mind would blank out and I would have to rethink everything she'd said before the lapse, while simultaneously trying to follow her current context. It wasn't easy.

"Remember the Principles of Vibration, and the *integrative period* when you have those lapses. It's the ultimate version of a learning curve," she said with a gentle smile.

Gloria's privy into my thoughts left me feeling embarrassed by the fact that there were no secrets between us. I also noticed that I felt at peace when I did understand something she said, but the lapses made me uneasy.

"A distorted sense of self causes suffering," she said, right on point. "The pathway to release from such distortion requires wanting it with all your heart, mind, and strength, and in trusting the Source of Life. This doesn't mean that you're to open yourself to, and accept what others tell you about their interpretation of God. It means to trust in the inspiration of your own heart and realization. In this trust, know that you are a holy creation."

The fluidity of meaning in Gloria's words was a soothing balm to my long-overworked brain.

"Surrender to the universe, look at yourself, and acknowledge what you find right there on the surface, Salvatore. You must fully accept and love yourself with all of your perceived flaws. If you hear a thought that says you could possibly be separated from God, acknowledge it as an *interject*. It's your inner voicing of a false belief you allowed someone, somewhere, at some time, to put into your head. Confront any such inner conflict and walk through it as if it were an open door. Do not define yourself by conflict, for that would be a lie, but walk through the door with the knowledge that you are an infinite, evolving soul in a universe that supports, rather than misleads you. Remember you are *in* the world, not *of* the world."

Fleeting sensations of a heretofore unknown sense of freedom flashed through me as Gloria conveyed this method of change. To be *in the world, but not be of the world* revealed so much in that moment. Tears rolled down my cheeks.

"Our Source is above the walls of man-made identities with their conflicting, self-protecting differences, my dear Salvatore" she said, after giving me time to compose myself. "Since we are extensions of our Source, we are also above those walls. The true purpose of religion is to gain insight into ourselves as evolving beings, but that *point was missed* somewhere along the line. For the most part, the world is in a holding pattern of reactivity involving fear; that fear is a reflection that its people don't know who they are."

Gloria was expounding on what the mystics had taught me. As I listened, I realized that there was a barrage of projections in my life, and that I really needed to look closely and intently to see what I was reflecting off the screen of life.

"As ever-evolving souls, people short themselves when they anchor their center of consciousness in the harmful beliefs visited upon them. None of these beliefs are a real part of their being, nor are they meant to stay, yet they are instilled and cultivated by so many who haven't truly searched their own hearts."

"I think it takes a lot of courage to face, and then dispel these types of interjected beliefs, especially because they serve fearful ideas about God." I dared to add my own interpretation.

"Of course it does, because you have to face everything holding those beliefs in place before you can let them go, and you hold them in place because they give you a sense of identity. But on the other hand, it's insane to think a belief has a life of its own, when *it is we, who are the life of belief.* When we gain insight into reasons not to hold a belief any longer, we withdraw its lifeline. However, dislodging, disintegrating, and dispelling core beliefs can be disorienting and fearful, since they are the cement of one's perceived identity. Although they might be false and distorted beliefs, they are held in higher regards than familiar old shoes."

At last, I was beginning to fully understand the concept of belief as something quite secondary. Also, it brought home, again, how people took their errant belief about themselves as Gospel.

"Yes, Salvatore, but their belief is far from Gospel," she interjected her response into my stream of thought, again. "Just remember, it's the natural action of the Absolute Reality ringing truly within that nudges any fear-associated belief to the surface so it can be dispelled. Instead of feeding beliefs that have the power to imprison you, exercise your ability to pass through them, and, into the light of understanding. Aspire to the truth about your identity, and you will surely be set on the road to the freedom you seek."

"Would it be correct to say that we find truth by considering our mental-emotional conditioning to be a negative investment of energy?"

"Salvatore, you're missing something here. Not all conditioning is negative in your judgmental sense of the word. Even unhealthy conditioning has value because you can learn from it at any stage in your development. Your ideas are limited, because they stem from a *good or bad* way of thinking that borders on resistance and self-debasement. But I am teaching you about self-acceptance and expansion. As far as any mental-emotional conditioning goes, you are free to keep what you want. At a point in your learning, what once seemed valuable to you may simply fall away as shed skin. There are no negative judgments from any God, only the ones you direct towards yourself. Your belief that there is something bad about you is evidence that you still revert to the tenets of fear-based religion."

Just when I thought I was beginning to understand everything Gloria was imparting, I was stunned by her admonition. Her observation meant that I wasn't nearly as free as I thought.

"But you *are* free, Salvatore!" She proclaimed excitedly. "You have yet to see the nature of your design. Your freedom isn't something acquired. You just need to be reminded to look in the direction of what reality has always been."

I felt naked when Gloria read my mind this time. It was deeply personal, probably because I was disillusioned and at a loss for words. I felt transparent as she continued to speak.

"As free-will-agents of electromagnetic energy, whatever someone internalizes as belief is exactly what he or she sees as life. Keeping in line with human intolerance of diversity, many scoff at people of different races, colors, creeds, and lifestyles, and out of convenience, people too often become pigeonholed into labels. Sadly, many of them internalize these assigned labels, and, inappropriately live up to them. Innumerable injustices occur daily because of conflicting personalities. All of this mishap is a result of the poison of ignorant thought. But when we practice universal laws of energy, we will come to understand our innate oneness, and justly promote reverence for all. In a world of inequalities, labels stunt growth, Salvatore; labels are but stew pots of stigma that the insecure use in an interdependent, yet intolerant society, with its overflowing prisons, mental institutions, and suicides."

I thought about people who believed in the labels placed upon them, and I knew I had to test myself to see where I had allowed for such manipulation in my life. The idea of pigeonholing and diminishing people in such a way raised questions about what it meant to be a *non-entity*.

The answer from within described a non-entity as one who is not the governing force of their creative potential as he or she experiences life, but, who instead lives solely through the thoughts and opinions of others, even to the extent of believing that they are separated from Omnipresence.

"The truth never changes," Gloria said. "All pleas for God's inclusion are meaningless because you were never excluded. Your freedom lies in waking from the hypnosis of your conditioning. Rather than becoming caught up in resisting any conditioning you don't like in yourself, it's best to acknowledge and accept it, so that you can move beyond it. Through this kind of allowing, you are opening yourself to the real you: a universal being who transcends conflict. Rise above unconscious humanity *that has given you the horror of war throughout every one of your generations*."

"Gloria, I can feel myself changing more and more as we speak and, quite frankly, it's a little unsettling, even disturbing. Sometimes I wish I had never started experimenting with the way I look at things," I said rather cautiously.

She looked at me as if I had two heads. "You've experimented with so much that led you nowhere, but to the dark night of your soul. You've witnessed loved ones engage in destruction of their bodies by substance abuse, and you've wandered onto that precipice yourself. Why wouldn't you test the deeper truths about you?"

I knew she was right, and I bowed my head and began to sob when I thought about my many friends who'd died so young.

Their mannerisms, personalities, and their tears, along with the sound of their voices and laughter were never far from my thoughts. Substance abuse may have taken them, but I knew that their enormous lack of knowledge was another reason for their absences. I also knew that I missed them terribly.

Gloria sat patiently and allowed me to indulge in my moment of grief before she continued.

"Knowledge would surely have benefited them," she stated, with an elevated kindness in her tone and appearance, "but there is also much *you* don't know. No one ends, Salvatore. Your friends are still in the classroom of life—just not in the same dimension as you. Your prolonged grieving weighs upon them. They will benefit when you stop it."

"You mean they know how much I miss them?" I cried.

"It would be better to say your grief anchors them, slows their progression."

"I don't understand. How could that be?" The thought that I've been keeping my friends tethered to this life took me to another level of grief.

"Why do you think you mourn, if not for the desire to keep them here? Your thoughts are a force directed at them. Remember, the universe is neutral."

"But I have only loving thoughts toward them." I stated, innocuously, trying to resist the truth.

"Alberto loved you, too. How else do you think he pulled you from your sleep before his transition? He knew enough in the end to let you go, though."

I shook my head. "I don't think I can ever forget them, Gloria."

"No one said you have to forget them. You can still love those who have moved on. Grieving and loving aren't the same. Do you recall times you thought you couldn't go on, even though you were unsure why you felt that way?"

I nodded. "Yes. Why did I feel that way?"

"Partly because there were people from your past who were holding onto you—people who loved you in other lives. You can help them all, Salvatore."

"How do I help them?" I was confounded with the idea of letting them go while still loving and remembering them.

"Think for a moment about God's *many mansions*, the physical dimension included. We all move on to other dimensional planes, and by learning to cease grieving the ones who have gone ahead, we also spread the powerful vibration of truth to those from our past who mourn us. The act is an example of the simultaneity of spirit, where giving is receiving. With this in mind, think about time. You might find it isn't what it seems."

I thought about time in the way she suggested, and I discovered that when two or more awakenings to a higher perspective happen simultaneously as the result of a single act, then there was less time—meaning, time had *collapsed* to a degree. I interpreted this phenomenon to mean that time appeared in exact ratio to our awakening, and also that the *end of time* is a highly evolved state. But I needed clarity concerning the matter of grieving for loved ones who'd passed on. "I see what you mean about time, Gloria, but how do we get to the point of fully accepting that there are other dimensions? I can't let go of grief, just from being told to do so."

"Open yourself to the larger reality of life, and temper grief by loving them even more. Love is truth, Salvatore, and the truth is that there is no end to life."

Her elucidation felt like a punch to my gut. "My head is spinning," I unabashedly confessed. "I feel at such a loss for who I am. I'm not most of the things I thought I was. I'm not even this body. You must realize how disorienting this is for me. It's as though the world's labels are made for a comfortable rut of sorts."

"Salvatore, calm down," she crooned. "You've made it

through more frightening changes that led you in the other direction, toward the negative pole. The depolarization you're feeling now is leading you closer to the positive pole. You will be renewed. Pass through what you're feeling with the truth as your guide. Remember—Perfect Love casts out fear. I will be here for you," she added, rather lovingly as a mother consoling an anxious child.

Her vibration lifted me, and I immediately thought of her as my *spirit mother.*

"All of the Great Masters have taught that freedom lies in looking beneath the surface activity of the mind. I will show you how to still your objective beta consciousness and go deeper into your subjective mind where you will resonate with the alpha frequency. While in this frequency, you will know the meaning of co-creation when you submit your desires to Universal Mind. You will see how free you've been in creating many of the circumstances you've experienced in your life."

"Thank you, Gloria. When we go into levels of subjective consciousness, are we supposed to ask for what we desire in the name of God?" I enquired, hungrier for more truths.

"What we've called God, really has no name as men do. The name of God *is* the frequency with which you will resonate. Ask the Great Spirit to help you recognize God's gifts that have been inherent in you from before your dream of time—the gifts that remain unalterable as time collapses."

"Thank you again. I will surely do so." I lowered my head with a deep sigh while pressing my palms into my cheeks to relax my face; it's a method I'd used many times throughout my life.

"The mystics have so much to teach you. You will learn specific vowel intonations geared towards activating the energy centers of your body-temple, particularly in connection to the pineal gland in the center of your brain. You will come to see that there is more to the endocrine system than what you know."

I immediately thought of Michael and the long "OM" he'd sent toward the ocean on the night we walked the beach together.

"As you learn to heal yourself, you will heal others—even from a distance. Your glands and autonomic nervous system, and the mechanisms performing beneath your awareness will prove to be invaluable as you awaken your ethereal body."

I began to understand that I had an ethereal body when I thought about the energetic components of light at the subatomic level of my physical body that Gloria had previously shown me. And, as expected, she picked up on my thoughts.

"The eye of your soul is beginning to open, Salvatore. The thankfulness you know now will pale in comparison to the gratitude you'll feel when you stop needing other's permission to be all of who you are. People don't realize how much they govern themselves by the opinions of others, because they still don't know themselves to be the Eternal Manifestation of the Unmanifest, Witnesses of the Absolute, and Sons of the Great All, whom you call God."

I had never heard a great truth said quite so beautifully. My trust in Gloria had become great. Being with her was turning out to be nothing less than a venture into the sublime. "I'm going to meditate on what you've given me, Gloria," I said with deep appreciation. "I feel relieved, and my strength is renewed just knowing I've been mistaken about such basic matters. But I still feel something unsettling stirring deep within me. I just can't put my finger on exactly what it is, though."

She chuckled softly. "It's alright, Salvatore. Soon you will understand why you feel this way. Don't worry. I'm with you, and I'm glad you will be meditating. It's good to use time to reflect on the truth you are shown. Turn weaknesses into strengths, and then use them as sounding boards to steer you toward wisdom. As you practice understanding the science of universal-natural law, acknowledge courage and persistence as fertilization for the seeds of change.

"Know and affirm what you want to bring into your life and to the world—not just by saying it. *Feel* the associated emotions, too! Your emotions are energized thoughts, and when infused into your intentions, they lead to the powerful vibration of faith that is the food of manifestation. Faith is ethereal, and it attracts celestial substances like itself through a duplication process in the plasticity of the universe. That which you think of regularly becomes the mantra of your faith, and it adds momentum to the manifestation of your will. This is why imagination is a treasure chest at your disposal. Draw from your sanctified imagination, Salvatore, for it is your greatest tool as a co-creator. It is also the importance of your knowing the Law, knowing your intrinsic part in the whole, and what you want."

Imagination. The very word itself had an uplifting chime as it opened up another dimension of understanding for me. "Gloria, since everyone is part of a Greater Whole, I understand how directing harm toward others, will actually bring harm to myself. This must be the basis for The Golden Rule, right?"

"Yes, but that's not all there is to it, Salvatore."

I noticed that Gloria's eyes had developed a greater depth to them than before. I felt rapturous, as though they were speaking inexplicable wonders to me. "What else could there be about The Golden Rule that I'm not seeing?" I asked, bewildered and excited at the same time.

"Living by The Golden Rule is a pathway that leads to more. Much, much more. You'll attract a more exalted state of being when you fully understand why it's best to treat others the way you would want to be treated if you were in their shoes. It isn't something I can explain with mere words."

As soon as she stopped speaking, I suddenly felt a stirring in the deepest part of my being. There was no wonder she couldn't show me with words. The little information she had verbally shared paled in light to what she was now communicating to me telepathically. I felt as if I'd been placed at the outer edge of the 'exalted state of being' to which she had alluded, and I could only describe it as a *holy moment*. I think I brushed the fringe of what has been called, *The Glory of God*, and to say it was beautiful, just wasn't enough. I was having a spiritual orgasm, many octaves higher than the physical kind; the two were related, although many degrees apart on a cosmic scale. There was no explosion, just a steady stream of incorruptible ecstasy that I sensed would carry me even higher. The feeling of complete safety was palpable, and as tears welled, I humbly lay down with both hands on my heart.

"Do you see what I mean, Salvatore?"

The sound of Gloria's voice pulled me back. I reluctantly withdrew from my exalted state, but remained in my physical position. Too choked to speak, I gazed at her and nodded.

"That was about as much of an influx of such high levels of vibration you can handle right now. You will adjust to it shortly. The mental, emotional, and physical aspects of your being need time to acclimate to this new and higher octave of vibration. This change was necessary to prepare you for the rest of what I have to show you. You experienced a merging of the masculine and feminine aspects of your being. You have seen this unity reflected in the physical dimension when two people join in relationships. But the day will come when the human race will evolve beyond physical genders, and relationships will be similar to what you just experienced. People are spiritual beings having a human experience, but you must remember that there is no physical gender in Spirit." She paused and then said, "You must rest for now."

As I rested, Gloria stood with her hands over her head, her palms facing upward. She then moved her hands downward pulling streams of light into her body from her head to her toes.

She approached me, knelt next to where I lay, and placed her right hand on my forehead and her left on my solar plexus. After ten, slow, deep inhalations and exhalations, she removed her hands and returned to her place.

Feeling replenished and ready to continue receiving from her fountain of wisdom, I stood to my feet, and noticed a distinct glow forming around her head as she began to speak.

"Many are misled when they fail to understand the universality of the power that animates us, and as a result, they sometimes use this power against others for selfish ends, unaware that, through the Law of Recompense, they are wielding it to their own detriment, as well."

I thought about my limited knowledge concerning the boomerang process, and then asked, "Would it benefit me to study electrical theory, magnetism, and the science of harmonics to understand how this all works?"

"Learning about science might afford you a high level of understanding. However, the mechanisms of the universe act together in your favor when you love the truth with all of your mind, heart, and strength, and, love your neighbor as yourself. The day will come when all people will know that they are priests of nothing—yet everything. Every single awakening to a higher reality will bring more and more joy to the greater whole. *This is what it means to be fruitful and multiply.*"

This new information from Gloria certainly turned the scope of my perspective in regard to being fruitful and multiplying, which I always thought was all about being prosperous and procreating. "How could we be priests of nothing, yet everything?" I asked. "I don't get it."

"As ministers of electromagnetic thought energy, your species has dominion over the earth. However, much of what you believe to be something, is really nothing, and what you believe to be nothing, could be the doorway to everything. Humanity's perception is clearly inverted, here. Surely, you are coming to understand this, no?"

"Yes, I do. For the most part… I think."

"Good enough. In the meantime, I suggest you take time to be still in mindfulness, and without resistance, acknowledge old patterns of thought that no longer serve you. Watch them pass like clouds without giving them your indulgence. Learn patience, as none of this is about force, but quiet practice."

"I will, Gloria. But I can't even guess where all of this will lead. I feel so small. Childlike," I said.

"One day, all sense of smallness will leave you. When it lives in alignment with the Cosmic Laws that govern all life, humanity will be lifted up and, behold its stance on the threshold of great change. At a critical point in mass-consciousness elevation, the vibration of the planet will shift to polarize in a higher octave. When Infinite Wisdom lights the earth, from the east to the west, mankind will have clear perception, and peace will blanket the world."

18

THE ILLUSION OF LOSS

*"I see God in every human being. When I wash the leper's wounds, I feel I
am nursing the Lord Himself. Is it not a beautiful experience?"*

— Mother Teresa

"Instability is common during transformation, and it occurs when the lies you have believed about your identity rise to be dispelled in the light of reality. You might think these untruths are only associated with painful experiences, but sometimes, even what we consider to be the good things of our lives, are really the result of hidden disturbances. For example, you could find yourself pursuing a vocation or a relationship that is unknowingly based on unresolved issues related to your self-image. These relationships might bring you some measure of joy and happiness; however, this so-called *bliss* you think you experience deserves a closer look. In doing so, you might find that the motivation behind your initial pursuit was grossly displaced, and you might develop the need to either change or walk away. A shift in perspective at this magnitude engenders a sense of loss. However, contrary to appearances, you are losing nothing, and time will show that you have gained immeasurably."

I was deeply enthused by Gloria's explanation of our distorted self-images driving our pursuance of relationships, or anything in life, for that matter. My own desire to make better choices that are directly related to my true identity increased at the idea of losing what we thought were 'good things', once enlightenment takes place. I needed further clarification, so I asked the sister, who'd so far demonstrated that she had all the answers.

"Gloria, when you referred to humanity as *priests of nothing*, did you mean that humans are blindly conducting lives that are based in illusion? The members of the churches I've attended, often said that we must all die to the self. I understand that they believed it meant forcing a change in one's behavior—change your ways—so to speak. But I get the feeling that 'dying to the self' is really about waking up and leaving an illusory sense of self behind. Is this true?"

"Yes, but that's a vague term since no one dies to anything. Let me clarify. What it means, is that as you awaken, the priest in you, or your Higher Self, has the ability to withdraw validity from a false idea of self. You can say that it's the validity to which you blindly gave power that dies. But in the purest sense, the validity was never real."

My thoughts raced to draw a diagram that I could follow. "So, if the validity was false, doesn't that equate an incorrect idea of self to something having no life, and therefore dead?" I asked.

"What do you think Jesus meant when he said, "Let the dead bury their dead", my dear Salvatore?"

A deep breath filled my lungs as Gloria redefined the meaning of the word *dead* by applying it to the mindset of those who were asleep to their true identity as universal beings. I had already learned that this fact was the real and only definition of sin. Becoming Self-Realized was tantamount to being Christed. This is what Jesus did. I listened attentively as Gloria continued to expound on the subject.

"Many mistakenly believe that dying to the self means that self-denial is the way to God, but in a world of duality, the opposite is true. Rather than look outward in your denial or resistance of self, *own the responsibility* to look within with the truth as your guide, and then advance through the walls of your identity. The erroneous ideas you have accepted will disintegrate when they are confronted with what is real. Since you are truth, extended from a Greater Truth, you have the ability to advance to this level of enlightenment; your presence here… now, is a Witness that it is possible.

"As you pass through the walls of your self-made prison, you are walking through the valley of the *shadow* of death; simply put, you are feeling the fear of an identity that doesn't want to die. When you emerge, you will know that the self-images with which you've identified for so long—and that appeared quite real to you —never truly existed; yet they were experienced. *The key here, is to realize that existence and experience are not the same.*"

I nodded, not from total comprehension, but from the recognition of a major fault in myself. "I think I live from both poles in this duality of ego and spirit, Gloria. It's like I'm serving two masters. Some people would call this sin."

"Most people live from both poles in the duality of life," she said, easing my anxiety. "The vacillation I explained earlier addresses this concept as the way to integrate new knowledge or to learn to walk the path of self-realization. However, you can't possibly *simultaneously* base your identity in both poles. That's what's meant by, *You cannot serve two masters.*"

The dichotomy confused me. "Can you tell me why it's impossible?"

"Of course. Here is an analogy: shadows on the wall at night may cause a child to become fearful, but when the child awakens to the light of day, or reality, the shadows disappear. Similarly, anyone who's aware of what's real has no reason to give value to, or live in accordance with what is not real. The dream is over!"

I nodded in unison with Gloria's last empathic exclamation as I thought about Michael, the only other person I knew who could bring meaning home to me like this. My mind was becoming so harmonious with all that Gloria bestowed on me that our resonance was like medicine to my soul.

"Gloria, I must admit that there were long periods of frustration when I couldn't embrace your precepts, to the extent that I thought my brain might explode. But your use of analogy helps in quenching my spiritual hunger. With that being said, could you please give me another analogy that would reinforce my comprehension of Oneness?"

Gloria smiled kindly at me. "I'm here to help you understand in whatever manner is most beneficial to you, Salvatore."

"Thank you, Gloria." I was grateful that she didn't think I was dense.

She nodded. "There exists a Substrate Reality that's similar to an infinite ocean where everything lives and moves, and has its being. This Substrate is *one pure energy* or *Holiness*. Think of this ocean as unending and crystal clear, with no divisiveness, not even within the diversity of its droplets. Now, imagine people as holy droplets of this ocean defining themselves by their differences, only because they lost sight of their ocean. Does any of this allegory ring any bells with you at all, Salvatore?"

"It leaves me thinking that I'm part of a mathematical equation," I said with indifference. "Despite the fact that I get the drift of what you're saying, I apparently perceive from a place of divisiveness because some words and opinions still seem to have more of an effect on me than others. I'm bothered when I hear preachers say that all people are sinners, but I'm not sure why."

"You feel this way because the word holds an accumulation of negative energy that's reflecting its own mistaken use. Sin literally means to *miss the mark* aimed at in archery. Since your very substance is an extension of holiness, the correct way to define sin would be to say that it's a sin to call yourself a sinner."

"Huh!" I uttered in response to this nugget of wisdom that needed to be shouted from every mountaintop in the world.

"As representations of thoughts, word symbols carry the energy inspired by the thinker. Because their human sources are extensions of Omnipotence, words become very powerful with whatever emotion infuses them. Think of them as energy mixtures, loaded with emotion that can significantly affect people in varying ways and degrees. Because of what it represents *in* falseness *to* falseness, fear of the word *sin* deters people from confronting their erroneous concepts and passing from ignorance into knowledge. The misused *sin* word with its satellite equations of death, guilt, fear, and loss, is the hallmark of over-identification with an incorrect sense of self and the three-dimensional world of form. You are not a sinner. You are holiness; yet a fragment of your mind has been extremely and detrimentally ingrained to think otherwise. Despite everything we've discussed, you *still* believe it, Salvatore! This is why you're often bothered by the opinions of misguided preachers, and of other people, as well."

Gloria's doubtful expression bothered me, but I knew it was less about her thinking I would be blind forever, and more about her desire to set me free, so I voiced my fears. "Thinking of myself as holy and not as a sinner seems like blasphemy, and it scares me, Gloria. So, if the concept you just explained isn't blas-phemy—as religious leaders define the word—what is blasphemy, and how can it be set apart as the only unforgivable sin?"

"There isn't anything outside of you that's causing fear. You simply have fearful thoughts that you've accepted from others. The definition of blasphemy is to be oblivious to the Omnipresence of The Holy Spirit. How can anyone know the meaning of forgiveness if they don't know the truth about their own being, about all other beings, and about *everything in existence* as being inseparable from The Holy Spirit, otherwise known as The Universal Intelligence? Nonetheless, mainstream religions and their offshoots still teach division. You can never be separated from God, Salvatore, nor can anybody or anything in creation be separated. This is an area of life where you either know, or you don't, where you are either hot, or cold. There is no lukewarm.

"You have studied the Bible," she proceeded in an impassioned voice. "To some degree, you must know that Jesus taught this topic in his message to elevate the thinking of humanity and, to save the world from its own adversity. Unfortunately, most were so conditioned by the thinking of his era that their minds weren't receptive to the truth. The words of Jesus, and other Ascended Masters who came to spread enlightenment throughout the ages, still go unheard by most in the world today. Through an obliteration of the truth found in biblical scriptures, there has been more carnage committed in the name of God than what could be addressed at the moment. But just as it was in the past, these current atrocities are centered around worshiping whatever version of ego projection is in operation at specific times."

Throughout my life, I have been plagued and pulled every which way by this fragment of mind and its fearful beliefs that Gloria described. I viewed this fragment, or lower feature of my ego with increasing clarity and my hope renewed when I learned how not to define myself by it. But I needed more guidance from my current spiritual advisor. "Gloria, would I be placing myself into a position to identify less with my physical body and ego if I attuned to the pure energy at the core of life, and live by The Golden Rule on a daily basis?"

"Yes, Salvatore." Her lips curled on a delightful smile. "You are learning to know what will strengthen you. The closer one aligns to what is real, the higher the expression of the "I" soul personality through the individuality of the "me". The evolution of the soul leads to vision through experiences on the physical and, other planes. The Masters have not attained full Self-Realization and knowledge of everlasting life as a reward for special acts of suffering or self-denial, but because they learned the higher laws of life, and know that all souls have within them the ability to know. That which lesser-evolved souls consider selfless degrees of sacrifice in service to humanity, are but illusions of loss. Furthermore, these illusions of loss are unknown in the minds of avatars, who came to teach the individual about the greater inter-connectedness of life as seen through a universal perspective. Students of the avatars, Jesus, Buddha, and Krishna, have formed religions dedicated to following their teachings. Although the outer forms of these religions may differ, the ultimate realization is the same, their teachings reflecting the era and the environment in which they lived."

"Speaking of avatars, why do so many people say that Jesus is the only way to truth?"

"Simply because they don't know any better. Although Jesus deserves great reverence, it's the Christ part we want, Salvatore—not the form of the man, Jesus."

In my understanding of scripture, I recalled that Jesus never asked, or wanted, to be worshiped. He always pointed toward the Father. I wondered if there was a comparison between Jesus' and other Great Master's teachings, so I asked, "Have all the Great Masters taught that there is no such thing as death and separation, and that holiness isn't acquired by some kind of sacrifice?"

"Yes. The Great Masters knew holiness isn't about making sacrifices to God. In the same light, spiritual unity isn't about separate bodies of people holding hands in any church. You see a compartmentalized world of form, only because you perceive from what you have compartmentalized in your mind. There isn't some *place* for unity. Unity is The Universal Intelligence within us;

it is beyond the idea of places. You *must* understand that unity is the continuum beneath all appearances where nothing can be lost. This Omnipresence cannot be sacrificed, and the belief that it can be stems from an upside-down point of view. You miss the lessons that avatars, like Jesus, teach when you only *see* from your limited point of view, and not from their level of mind."

Her statement made me think about death and how it might be viewed in regard to letting go of illusions. "Does what appears to be death, occur only because of limited vision?" I asked.

"Or no vision at all," she swiftly argued. "Only a false mindset believes in death, but what is false has no life and doesn't exist. Think of yourself as two selves for a moment—a false idea of self and a Real Self. What proceeds from falseness is only false and unreal, or nothing at all. Likewise, what springs from the real is always true, part of everything, and eternal. The line of thought originating from a false idea of self is in line with the idea of death, *because it is dead*. The unreality of the temporal world will pass away along with false identities. But souls are real and eternal, and identities will be transmuted. I remind you of this, not because I am judging the world as bad, but because so many believe their perception of the world's ways of thinking as solid and set, when they are not."

Gloria broke down some stubborn barriers with her last transformative outpouring. Clearly, it was in perfect accordance with reality. Her finesse with words enriched my sensibilities in all areas. My mind gravitated to the subject of Jesus because he was part of my life to a large extent. The churches I attended portrayed him as a dual personality—one who could love unconditionally, yet who could also be disdainful. Gloria's description of him was completely different. I liked and, trusted her interpretation, so I asked her to speak more about him.

"Jesus' presence on earth was the embodiment of The Universal Intelligence at the foundation of Creation," she began.

"He was, and is, a fully conscious interdimensional being. His crucifixion was an attempt by lower minds to make division where there can be none. His resurrection symbolized that *Life never dies, and that the idea of death comes from the dead or a blind perspective held in a field of unrecognized unity.* Look closely at what this means, and ask yourself if you aspire toward Life, or if you serve fear, death, and everything else the illusion of separation offers."

Thoughts about the horrors done to Jesus flooded my mind. Yet, he forgave his killers. The idea of his forgiveness exasperated me, especially since as Gloria pointed out, those who crucified him, and much of the world, to this day, still don't understand the symbolism of his death, nor his resurrection. "My mind still fluctuates, Gloria. I have difficulty retaining some of the things you say. I can't even get past forgiveness after watching the news on television, let alone grasp the concept of eternal life. The idea of forgiving seems logical when you explain it, but it shrinks when I hear about one person committing unthinkable acts against another. I don't understand why everyone is expected to forgive. There are dangerous people in the world who commit horrible crimes. I wouldn't want to be anywhere near them. Why should they be forgiven?"

"Salvatore, Christ is a high state of awareness. To be in Christ is to know forgiveness because you understand it, as opposed to offering a rote act. You must come to understand that forgiveness is more than a nicety some express as the right thing to do. *Forgiveness is a knowing* that comes as people move closer to realizing their true identity as eternal souls. If you don't know yourself in the universal sense, you may choose not to forgive, but if you could see what forgiveness actually is, and does, there simply is no doubt that you would forgive. Think of forgiveness as a bridge with one part in this world, the other in the next, and All Power giving rise to the one thought to build the bridge."

"I'm trying, Gloria. Truly I am." Since I assumed that the

purpose of my journey was to understand as much as I possible could, I took a deep breath and exhaled slowly in an effort to calm my growing anxiety. "Where does the ego fit in with forgiveness?" I asked upon feeling a bit calmer. "Does the ego forgive, and is it also forgiven?"

"Listen closely. The lower ego believes it forgives and that it's forgiven, but because the ego has no essence in the Cosmic, it cannot know anything about forgiveness either way; therefore, the lower ego, or the identification with a limited sense of identity doesn't truly exist. Like a dream, it is experienced with no knowledge of the Greater Whole."

"But Gloria," I exclaimed as my mind became in a fog of confusion, "I thought it was the bad things done through ego that are forgiven. How then can the ego personality not know forgiveness?"

"The things that the ego calls sins and that it believes it forgives, are not sins, but an effect of sin. They are a chain-reaction based in the one root sin, which is the belief in the ego-identity itself. An egoic mindset that thinks it forgives is actually attempting to validate itself. This is what religions with man-made rules do to people. But *true forgiveness is the recognition of the soul,* over and above the reactive ego. So, it's not acts that are forgiven, Salvatore. *Acts, as evil as they can be, are but mirrors of sin.* Conscious souls understand forgiveness because they correctly define themselves and others. They sense the unlimited, and know that we are all holiness as extensions of singularity. The full realization of the truth will bring about the end of the root sin of ego identification, and all other errors that identification had projected onto the screen of life will collapse."

Gloria had distinctly implied that the definition most people gave to sin needed to be reinterpreted. This entire line of thought was a reversal of the way most of the world viewed life. It left me feeling as if I had no grip on anything. "Gloria, a part of me feels that I'm being pulled into a dawning sense of unification, even though the universe is neutral. I feel like I'm either being dragged, weighed down, or held back. What does it mean? Why do I feel this way?"

"You will be fine, Salvatore," she assured me with a smile. "The universe is just becoming what it is. Be assured that you're doing your part. When people exercise mental tools that help them see beyond the frozen, false self-images they bought from the world, and then move into knowledge of the soul, they will be free from delusion. This is your process. You need only acknowledge it. Forgiveness isn't about accepting malevolent acts, and you needn't place yourself in proximity to murderers nor anyone who intends harm. Forgiveness is about moving beyond the world's mistaken interpretation of sin. Even as infinite beings, the world's human inhabitants aren't able to evolve past that mistake until it's seen for what it is and released to oblivion.

"It's a form of insanity to deny your surface mind knowledge of the multidimensionality of your soul; many think they are sane in this, because there are multitudes of others who are like them. The power of agreement is poisonous in this regard. Forgiveness mends the misperception of your split, separated mind that believes only in its will, so pray you learn to understand it without delay. Know that a falsely conditioned fragment of mind truly has no will at all, and that forgiveness moves you away from that mind and activates memory of the soul. Once you cross the bridge of forgiveness, the veil that obscures the absolute reality that *WE ARE the Will of God*... is removed."

Gloria clasped her hands together and became quiet, giving me time to reflect, I supposed. I was moved by the profundity of what she conveyed, but it still hadn't sunk in entirely. With further introspection, I learned that my autonomous fragment of mind was activating in the background. It seemed to have put up block-ades to prevent everything I was learning from taking hold, which was no surprise, since the information was directly related to its undoing.

My ego-identity had tentacles that ran throughout my personality, and that identity—my sense of "I"—felt threatened, and it didn't want to let go. This supposed self, this tiny spot on infinity, was fighting tooth-and-nail to be in control. The part of me that stepped back and witnessed this scenario knew that this fragment of my mind wasn't really me, and so it began to infuse that knowledge into my psyche.

"Salvatore, breathe through all unsettling thoughts and emotions coming to the surface," Gloria said in a smooth, serene tone. "Yes, it's the defensive walls of your ego protecting itself. Don't resist. Simply breathe, acknowledge what's coming up, and continue to pay attention to what I'm saying to you."

I already knew that Gloria could read my mind, so I wasn't surprised at her insertion into my thoughts, and at this point, I really didn't care. I gave her a nod of acknowledgement and then resumed our talk about universal design. "The thought of a loving Source, rather than an angry God bent on punishing sins is quite relieving, Gloria, especially to the Catholic boy in me, who later found himself in a Pentecostal Church."

"Remember that when you hear about vengeance being the Lord's, it's not about an angry God. It's a misnomer for the Law of Recompense. As electromagnetic beings, our thoughts, words, and actions are actual charges of energy. Never forget that everything we think, say, and do, attracts energy like itself as it travels through the loop. And because the universe is a unified field, our thoughts, words, and deeds return to us like a boomerang, more powerful than when first transmitted."

"Is the Law of Recompense the channel through which we're punished for wrongs, then?"

"No, Salvatore. That idea is from the dogmatic thinking in you. The function of this Karmic Law of Cause and Effect is to lead us to know ourselves through a natural feedback-loop-system. Conscience is developed through this system. The universe is just, and the Law of Recompense is justice shining a light on error. At some point, we will feel remorse when we experience the pain our mistakes inflicted on others. The light is always working behind everything to rectify, not bring punishment. The Law works both ways, so we also reap the rewards of our service. Recognition of our innocence is the ultimate justice. There is no place to hide in this infinite matrix, not even your thoughts. Despite the illusion of time and distance, energy never really leaves its source. There really is no place else for it to go."

Humankind has a tendency to project its finite ideas in hopeless attempts to define our Infinite Source. In their backward perspective, they are yet to grasp that our Source is beyond description—yet it is what defines us.

Gloria added that all internalized belief systems that promoted judgment led to self-imposed obscurity or *hell*. She also said that the pain it generated was a call for mankind to learn to take responsibility for our own thinking.

"I'm glad you're listening, Salvatore. The answers you seek are in your questions. I will transpire our discussion to you directly, wordlessly, and ask that you practice focusing on what rings with certainty within you. As beings of truth, we elicit a distinct response when we touch into what is real. *We know when we know.*"

Gloria paused for a moment, and looked at me lovingly as she'd done many times during our conversation. I felt so attuned to her, like she was part of me.

"When I reprimanded you as a boy," she said, somewhat remorsefully, "I was under the power that I had given to illusion. In the ensuing years, I tore down the walls of a false identity, and was delivered to greater understanding. My eventual transition brought me to a dimension of a higher vibration close to yours.

From there, I was able to adjust my frequency to be even closer to your plane. This is why you see me as translucent. Now, I must warn you that our journey will escalate since I have many things to show you. I will lead you to see life in yet another way, and you will come to know there is nothing new under the sun."

Gloria slowly turned away and rested her hands on her heart. She tilted her head slightly, and as she brought her gaze upward, an exquisite light revealed the contour of her face. This image stunned me, because it was a replica of Mother Mary's pose, depicted in a painting on my grandmother's bedroom wall.

THE UPPER ROOM

"Look at every path closely and deliberately, then ask ourselves this crucial question: Does this path have a heart? If it does, then the path is good. If it doesn't, it is of no use."

— Carlos Castaneda

When she met my gaze again, Gloria's eyes bore directly into mine as they'd done during our very first meeting when I still had no idea why she'd appeared to me. The gap between our minds had diminished remarkably; I now understood that it was illusory, and had only appeared to be there because of my ego-identity consciousness. She permeated me with information through an extraordinary mode of communication, and what she conveyed was clear, as were all things in this field of Oneness. She explained that we would gradually continue to rise and ascend into a higher octave of vibration on this journey.

She then led me to what was called *The Upper Room*. The best way to describe the experience would be to say that it transcended beyond explanations and expanded into the fringe of an ultimate reality. All sense of well-being I'd ever known paled in comparison to the opulence that was now lilting through me. I felt like I was floating in the pastels of dusk above the low whistle of buoys that had lulled me to sleep nightly when I was a child. Beauty swept through me and gently transported me into boundless ecstasy. "Is this love that I'm feeling, Gloria?" I asked, breathlessly.

"Yes, Salvatore, but it's merely a glimmer of what awaits you and all of humanity. Take away the illusions of the world, and love is all that is left. This universal love is the cohesive property of Omnipresence. It is complete, eternal, and more powerful than that which the world knows as love. It is a blending of everything righteous, pure, and sacred, and has no unfulfilled desire to be loved in return. You still don't understand that you are love."

As Gloria had promised, we ascended into another higher octave of vibration.

I knew that I was experiencing my First Conscious Holy Communion when The Holy Symbols reappeared as reflections of Absolute Reality living within me. They came directly from the Source of Life at the core of all being where holiness lives. There were Symbols of love, faith, charity, forgiveness, truth, humility, gratitude, grace, reverence, and many more. As representations of innocence, they moved me beyond belief, and into the knowledge that we ARE innocence.

I referred to The Holy Symbols as *first words*, because they superseded the cluttered energetic grid of the world's ordinary words. They were more definitive than human's mundane, burdensome word symbols that often lose clarity through a labyrinth of clouded thinking, mistranslations, and projections. The message of the Holy Symbols of Truth was that the key to everything is to *know thyself*.

While in the glory of the upper room, my viewpoint changed, and it became plain to see that our overlay of human belief and conditioning were the very things that blinded us. But even though we have blind mindsets acting in default, this isn't an error. I was shown that what appears as error actually stems from a foundational aspect of Creation where the *One* of Singularity extended to *Two* in order to comprehend Itself through a counterpart, for a necessary contrast of darkness occurred with the Two away from its home. We are the Two awakening to the ONE we are. There is no other way for Singularity to experience Itself, except through the glory of our awakening. All life is a holy unfolding.

I began to understand space and time as tools for humanity's evolution, and that they didn't exist as absolutes.

"Don't confuse yourself with an offset view of space and time or by trying to figure them out scientifically," she explained. "They are the same, and intrinsic to the steeping of your organic senses into the thought systems with which you identify. Space and time serve as stepping-stones that will unwind naturally when you come to understand linear perception from beyond the interpretations of the body senses."

She also informed me that I was sufficiently attuned to handle the next level of our inter-dimensional rendezvous.

"I have come to you as a medium to assist your highest guardian, who is of a timeless dimension. Neither of us is capable of receiving direct communication from this entity whose knowledge is too high a vibration for our level of evolution.

"This being is so far removed from the concepts of the physical dimension, that access to you has been through your insights, sensations, and light experiences—much like the one you had in your room, and through a distinctly answered prayer concerning your mother. Also, by using me as a channel to speak during this divine intercession.

"The three entities with me are also of a higher realm, and they are here to help stabilize the vibration of this inter-dimensional convergence. As a child, you were able to see one of them as the great Chief he was during a previous lifetime. After the order of your higher ethereal guardian, he is powerful, and has infused you with energy during your trying times. He bridges the gap between you, your highest guardian, and me."

As I listened to the alternating tones in her voice, I was beginning to realize that not only did Gloria know everything about my life in detail, but that she also felt all the emotions of my experiences.

"The physical manifestations that you, as a co-creator breathed life into, are similar to how the seven colors of the crystal I gave you during our initial encounter are a *translation* of your ethereal guardian. Salvatore, you have attracted a celestial servant of the highest order—Saint Gabriel the Archangel."

I felt time stand still at Gloria's revelations to me. She also told me that my powerful guardian, Chief Great Blue Mountain, had created the crystal in ancient time out of substances from the higher dimensions, and has since been its caretaker. Gloria also said that he had the ability to will the crystal to himself whenever he felt the need to use it. She explained its necessity in the transference of immeasurable frequencies through the celestial realms that would make the visitation of the Archangel Gabriel possible.

I slowly retrieved the crystal from my pocket and I placed it between us. A cathartic sensation rose from within as a wind of unspeakable love blew through me, and carried with it the memory of an early winter morning from five months before. The memory detailed my awakening at the usual time of 4:30 a.m. to get ready for work. But instead of getting out of bed, I rolled over to face the large window of the old brick building where I resided at the time.

As I lay there, dumbfounded, I saw silvery-white beams of light streaming downward through the window at about a 45-degree angle, as though through holes in a pegboard. There were no coverings on the window, much less pegboards, and I watched this light for a minute or so before rolling over to face the opposite wall.

My gaze landed on a closet door that I believe I was viewing at a molecular level since it appeared to be crawling with ants. There were no ants; the door's substance was moving. I turned again to face the window. The light was still there, but within a minute, it slowly faded like the effect you get when turning off ballpark floodlights. I turned toward the closet door again and saw nothing unusual. Then I looked back at the window. The light had returned, but then, once again, it gradually faded.

I rose to investigate, but there was nothing but the silent rawness of a cold dawn outside. I asked myself if anything I'd ever known could cause such light to shine through the second-floor window. The answer came back as a distinct, "*No!*"

I set out to work that morning, thrilled with an apparent newness of eyesight. When I got to my workstation, I noticed that I didn't need my reading glasses to magnify the tiny laser-scribed identification numbers on the silicon wafers I fabricated. This sharpness of vision lasted for two days, then my impaired sight returned, and once again it became impossible for me to read anything without my glasses.

There was no doubt that I had been wide-awake during the light experience in my room, to which Gloria had alluded. The prayer for my mother, that Gloria also mentioned, was surely answered.

My mother had Multiple Sclerosis. One day, I sat on the edge of my bed and went into an unusual audio-visual and emotionally charged meditation. My reflections led me to recall many early childhood experiences with my mother. During this loving focus, which included smiles, laughter, and a tear or two, I felt a receptive presence sit next to me on my bed.

I felt no fear, and after asking this presence to touch my mother with healing, I closed the prayer, and went off to work. I forgot about the prayer quickly, and didn't even recall it on the following day, when Mom called to tell me about her experiences on the previous day—the day I'd visualized her healing.

Mom recounted that she'd been sitting in her recliner watching television, when she became increasingly annoyed by a strange, oscillating hum growing louder and louder in her ears. Upon standing, she was alarmed by a feeling of intense heat, accompanied by the sensations of pins-and-needles running up and down her body. Mom told me that she'd feared she was having a stroke.

Attempting to trace the origin of the sound, she removed her glasses, thinking they were interfering with the volume control of her hearing aid. When that didn't help, she removed the hearing aid, and was relieved when the annoying humming immediately stopped.

Her voice rang with excitement when she'd told me that her hearing had become as clear as a bell. She also said that she was able to read the small print on the television screen without her glasses. "I've *never* been able to do that!" she'd exclaimed.

Her voice boomed when she told me of her plans to buy a rowing machine so she could begin an exercise regimen to ward off the effects of MS. Her buoyancy lifted me, yet I failed to connect the dots that all of this happened on the day before, at the same time I prayed on my bed.

After I spoke to her, I went to work at my commercial cleaning job. When I walked into the empty building that night, the memory of the prayer, and of my mother's phone call, hit me like a ton of bricks.

In the abruptness of the moment, three entities stood before me. I recognized one as the presence who'd sat next to me on my bed during my prayer. It was becoming apparent that they'd come to remind me of my lack of expectation for Mom's healing, even to the degree of total forgetfulness.

At the same time, these entities told me that my emotional prayer, focused visualization, and the letting go of it through forgetting, was what sent it hurtling toward my mom. They said I just happened to forget too thoroughly. I wondered if they had appeared to scold me, to tell me that prayer isn't just a feel-good-game, and that I should pay attention? They acknowledged that I had prayed "correctly", but that in the end, I hadn't even noticed the results. I felt admonished.

Spiritual entities don't use words with me, and they don't appear as solid, yet I distinctly feel them in dimensions beyond the three common ones of the physical. They convey rapidly through pure thought and feelings that I dilute in my struggle with words.

They'd left me shaken by their directness, but before departing like the wind, they'd assured me that there is life after what we perceive as death, and that, _yes_—they were really present. Not to be disrespectful, but it would be more accurate to say that they shoved it into my face.

I have no regrets about the experience. It taught me that it's unnecessary to beg the universe for anything, and that depending on circumstances beyond what I could know, healing will, or won't happen. While praying, I had begged, _Please just touch my mother with healing!_ And she was partially healed. I do wish, though, that I had simply asked for my mother's complete healing, because the actual outcome was an exact duplication of my request.

ANGEL OF THE HIGHEST ORDER

"One's aim should be to concentrate and simplify, and so to expand one's being... and so to float upwards towards the divine fountain of being whose stream flows within us."

— Plotinus

"There is great love in our midst, Salvatore. I have felt love, but never have I been in harmonic vibration with such high entities, who actually know and exude divine love, as now."

Gloria's voice seemed to have blended with the harmonic vibration around us; it was serene and melodious to my ears. The crystal I had set between us earlier was now activated with the seven colors of the spectrum, so the thought to speak didn't enter my mind. The rays appeared to play off each other, expanding greatly, upward, and outward. Despite all its beauty, the world had nothing to compare.

Great Blue Mountain, the Indian Chief of my childhood, glowed as a holographic image with many alternating faces within a pillar of the light. To my amazement, some of the faces belonged to people from my past—people who were pivotal to my life. One looked like Michael before it morphed into Gloria's face. I even thought I saw my own image. Was my mind playing tricks on me through some optical illusion? Unsettling feelings began to rise, but they were quickly quelled by another relaxing infusion, similar to the one I had previously received from Great Blue Mountain.

He raised his hand and brought forth heartfelt images of Incline Village, the enchanted world that Jack and I had visited near Lake Tahoe, two years earlier. Ancient scenes flowed through my mind's eye, and I proceeded to relive segments of an antediluvian lifetime.

Back in those times, the tribes of the High Sierra's knew that the harshness of the elements would take its annual toll. To my amazement, it became clear to me that this lifetime was mine, and that Jack was my son. Looking through this window to the past, I saw that spring had been our sacred time of ritual, during which we expressed thankfulness for our safety as we looked toward the incline next to the lake—the place where our people made shelter. Back then, emotion was magnified because we knew the environmental odds were against us. Our tribe was solid. We relied heavily on one another, and were so close-knit that we shared the meaning of our dreams with each other. I felt deeply sentimental while watching these scenes.

When the brutality of the following winter began to play out, Great Blue Mountain brought revelations about this past life to a close, but not before I realized that Jack and I had perished—as did much of the tribe—while we huddled together at the end of a prolonged struggle against the elements.

I stood there on the stairwell landing, in awe of the historical images Great Blue Mountain had brought forth, knowing that when Jack and I had visited the magnificence of Lake Tahoe, two years prior, we'd been somehow drawn to this remarkable place.

The soulful sensations Incline Village held for us, bled through during our visit many moons later. It was as though we had come full circle in some inexplicable way.

The Chief, Gloria, and I, stood bathed in the light of sages from beyond time. I would have been fine staying in this state for a longer period of time, but that was not to be the case.

Gloria spoke softly, yet forthrightly. "Chief Great Blue Mountain has been with you for many lifetimes, and in extraordinary ways. Know that this is a joyous occasion for him." She placed her hand on my forearm, and with an earnest expression in her eyes, she continued. "You and I have a traumatic event in common that involves the same person in the physical dimension. I have healed my wound, but for reasons of survival, which you will come to understand, the events you suffered lay beneath your conscious awareness. Nevertheless, the consequences of the injustice done to you are the roots of much strife and, the reason for the inner conflict you have felt for most of your life. You suffered mental anguish that no child should have to bear. That child still lives within you. My being heals with you at other levels through the Archangel Gabriel's virtue that is transformed into the light of this crystal."

Gloria closed her eyes and grew silent in her devotion for a few moments. Eventually, she turned to me and said, with a level of awe in her voice, "Not only are we in alignment with the vibration of Truth, but Truth is pulling us into Itself through the Law of Attraction."

"What traumatic event are you talking about, Gloria?" I asked, perplexed.

"Do you trust in God, Salvatore? Do you believe God is with you and could never abandon you?"

"In accordance with my studies with the mystics and with the weight of all that has happened up until now, yes, I do trust and believe in God."

"What you have been learning has directed you to one place in your psyche, but you've kept yourself from going further in self-discovery. Though you have experienced the Holy Symbols and tasted glory, you are still conceptualizing rather than experiencing when it comes to the truth about your own life."

"I thought this was all about applying new concepts to my life and realizing the world is basically a labyrinth of compounded conditioning reflecting off each other."

"You're correct, but how can you apply new concepts to your life when you don't know your life? You don't remember some things, Salvatore. But still, these things have had their affect. Your sight is distorted. You feel threatened by your surroundings, yet the world isn't bad or evil, in itself. Although there are negative experiences through the misuse of power, the world is still subject to your potential and can be beautiful. Retreating from the world to look inward for healing, only to turn your attention outward again to escape a sense of fear, leaves you nowhere. Can you see where you are required to go now?"

"I still don't understand, Gloria. I'm not well with any of this. I think I'm going to be sick," I said, as my heart began to race.

"You are confused and frightened at the mention of going within. There is a reason for this. Can you tell me what it is?"

Gloria wasn't looking at me objectively. She was fully present as a part of me, and the love on her face was almost palpable in the air between us. Startled into silence while looking at her, I paused before speaking again. "No, Gloria. I... I can't tell you. I know you mean well, but I feel defeated, and like I've failed greatly in some way. I thought we were on a journey, and that more would be revealed to me, but none of this seems to make sense, anymore. I'm not sure I understand what you're asking. All I know, is that I feel apprehensive to the point of being ill." I grew pensive, and my vision blurred. I shifted my body and held my head in my hands in an effort to calm myself.

"The journey is yours to take," Gloria said, softly. "You're the one who must do the revealing. You are the sentinel standing at the gateway to your consciousness. The decision to accept anything into your mind is always yours, even when you are too young to know what's best. Likewise, it's up to you to dispel from your mind what doesn't serve you. No healing is accomplished by proxy at that level of discernment. The discernment all comes down to you. Your old beliefs are beginning to dislodge as we speak. There are incongruities that cannot survive truth. They will rise to the surface of your mind and begin to flow inside of you like debris afloat on the fountain of living waters."

Whatever that debris was, it had made my life tumultuous. I had prayed so much, often questioning if anyone was listening.

"You chose a path of new knowledge, and have come to this point in your mystical studies because the trauma you experienced as a child caused an imbalance in your psyche. You were shamed, and shame is the lowest, most detrimental energy on the emotional-tone-scale. Your trauma, like all traumas, was based in error, which compounded over time, and drove you to the soul-level of your triune being with heartaches and questions. Simply stated, Salvatore, you asked for clarity in a loud way, and now you are receiving it. Imbalances are a call to balance."

Although Gloria's words were meant to calm and encourage me, I was becoming increasingly more unsettled inside, even disoriented.

"We come to know truth through stillness. Yet the vibration of truth is loud—not audibly loud—but distinct in such a way that when diligently sought, the quest appears quite evidently in the higher dimensions as a light-formation. Seeking the truth is a prayer that reverberates throughout the universe. The high entities who see the petition answer it. For them, it's an act of the highest calling.

"Your prayers were heard, Salvatore. Go towards the unconditional love of divinity, just the way you are, with all your perceived flaws. In fullness to your own being, you have yet to apply the ways of healing through the truth that is shown to you and which you have contemplated."

"I can't stop shaking, Gloria," I said in an unsteady voice as everything inside me seemed to crumble. "I feel light-headed, like I'm outside of my body listening to myself talk. I don't understand what's happening." I stood trembling, as layer-after-layer of emotional intensity began ripping through my nervous system. I fluctuated between feelings of fear, anger, and helplessness—and then indifference.

"You've disconnected emotionally from the situation, Salvatore. Look at me."

I looked at her and swallowed as I seemed to become choked on all the emotions rioting inside me.

"Know nothing in you can turn me away. Know that I am here, and that you are doing the best thing, although it may not seem so. Now, bring back your emotional body," she gently admonished.

Gloria's face was almost transparent in this light, but I saw the reassurance she offered me. I tried to speak, but every word was slurred. My face and tongue were numb, and my distorted vision made me think that my eyes were misplaced in my cranium. All equilibrium in me was lost. But evidently, I realized that I had followed her direction and brought back my emotional body, since I was now feeling extreme agitation, followed by an internal wailing, deep within the core of my being.

"You are moving into a place within yourself where fear is surrounding occurrences pivotal to your identity-construction that, at one time, was formulated in accordance to your beliefs," Gloria said. "Acknowledge the fear as a call to interface what is hidden with what is known."

She paused, as if giving me time to accept what was

happening to me before she continued. "Your young mind knew no choice in how to react after something grossly detrimental happened to you, so the fear developed as a barrier to guard and defend what needed protection in your time of need. Just as your skin will form a scar when healing a wound, and then a callous against repeated assaults, your mind will unconsciously protect itself by employing defense mechanisms when necessary. Both cases serve as survival because the mind-body unit responds only to its ability to interpret circumstances.

"In the same way that there can be an overabundance of scar tissue in the body that form adhesions, unresolved fear creates more of itself. The only way to complete the process of resolution is to interface what is true with what has been set apart in a cocoon of fear. The last victory for those of the physical dimension will be to relinquish the fear of death, which will come for you at a later time.

"For now, I am with you—guiding your every step. I won't abandon you. But I must ask you to summon your courage, take up your sword of truth, and without turning back, face whatever fearful thoughts rise in your mind. You hesitate, because you have done this before, only to experience a violation of your trust by those you believed in most. There will be no such irreverence here," she assured me.

Gloria lit frankincense, which for some reason, immediately caused me to freeze with terror.

My uncontrollable shivering grew to awkward jerking motions when another vision screen appeared and enveloped us. As I was pulled into a stream of images, I saw a pale-faced priest walking briskly toward his change room in a church. I gasped, then shouted, "I'm not safe, Gloria! Please don't let him get me."

I heard the sound of Gloria's voice in prayer, along with a multitude of other invisible beings. Their prayers glowed and appeared to ascend like fine threads of silk, when in an embodiment of compassion, she held my hand, and whispered, "And this, too, shall pass."

The priest emerged from his change room. I watched as he strode impatiently up the aisle. The clacking of wooden rosary beads suspended from somewhere within the folds of his loose, black garb, and the sound of his heels striking the floor pierced the silence. When he arrived at his place in the confessional, beads of sweat began dripping from my brow.

The light of the crystal rose farther upward and shone ever brighter upon my arrival to what turned out to be, a crossroads of truth and illusion in my young life. Reassurance infused me when Chief Great Blue Mountain's form, encased in a pillar of light, became illuminated in a glorious transfiguration of the Archangel Gabriel.

My beloved Gloria became nearly invisible when the priest closed his door. The power of belief would become evident as she helped me relive scenes on the screen of my life, from when I was eight years old.

SIN OF THE FATHER

"The privilege of a lifetime is to become who you really are."

— Carl Jung

G loria stayed with me while the screen of my life remained open. She motioned for me to focus on what I was seeing and feeling. I did as she asked.

I sat in the church, holding my *Little Child of God* book that was given to me in Sunday school where I studied for my First Holy Communion. I believed it was imperative for me to confess all my sins to the Father in the confessional, or else I'd go to hell. I recalled the picture hanging on my grandmother's bedroom wall that showed people on fire, their hands reaching up from the flames of the devil's domain. I recalled how I had focused on the pain on their faces and their silent pleas, back then.

Grieving for them, and scared for myself, I had fully believed that when death came, I would be sent into the same fire. Authority figures in my life had told me that whenever I was bad, it was like putting a black mark on my soul and stabbing God in the heart. Not only was I convinced that I was bad, but I also experienced a lingering feeling that suggested there was a well of something unforgivable in me because I'd believed, by then, that my soul was full of black marks. Thoughts about God brought only fear and the darkness of uncertainty. At eight years old, I knew no better. Worst of all, I had a festering wound inside me.

In preparation for my First Holy Communion, I understood that when I did something wrong, all I had to do was confess it to the priest. He would talk to God for me. Then he would give me penance to say at the altar to ensure my absolution, which would get me off the hook, but only if I was truly sorry. So, with self-loathing and paralyzing fear, I sat in the church on that cold night in silence, nauseated by the pungent odor of frankincense.

While waiting for my turn to go into the confessional, I languished in the belief that there was still a chance God wouldn't forgive me because I was too bad, and had too many black marks on my soul—not to mention, I believed I had somehow stabbed him many times. I thought about the eyes of Jesus in the picture hanging on the wall at home. They followed my every move with disdain. What would happen in the confessional? What was to become of me? My heart was pounding.

Anticipation ran rampant to a point nearing hysteria. All of my trust had to be placed in the priest. He was to be the mediator on my behalf. There was simply no way out. I wasn't ready, only courageous, when the door to the confessional opened.

My head spun as I rose from the pew. Placing one foot in front of the other, I was drawn into the darkness of the booth. While kneeling before this priest, I gave all my power over to him. Appearing as a shadow in the dark, he recited his introductory prayer to me. I responded dutifully with, "Bless me Father, for I have sinned…"

There were no signs of safety coming from this priest. His demeanor was as cold as the statues in the church on that winter night. Despite his hasty aloofness, I slowly bared my innermost secrets to whom, I thought, was his holiness: "And these are my sins: I stole two Chunkies, a Hershey Bar, and a Reese's Peanut Butter Cup from Sterling's Drug Store. I disobeyed my parents, used swear words, and haven't been to church or confession in the five months since I received my First Holy Communion."

The Father's stern reaction confirmed my worst fears. Thoughts, that I was likely to be lost to the devil, loomed large. How was I to tell him the rest? Terror-stricken as I was, my need to get rid of the dirty feelings I bore drove me to continue.

"Is there anything else?" He asked, impatiently.

Although it seethed inside, I was yet unable to tell him what had happened to me the previous summer while walking home from the beach one day. I was saving what I thought to be the worst for last.

I felt Gloria caress my shoulder lovingly as tears streamed down my face. The realization that she was feeling this experience along with me drew sobs from deep within my gut. What I didn't know, was that her presence would soon open me to a yet higher understanding, that would transpose upon the traumatic *pseudo-confession* of my childhood being played out before us in this vision.

As a child growing up in Gloucester, I used to ride my bike to the waterfront so I could watch my relatives work in the fish-processing plants. I wanted to work alongside them, but I couldn't because, of course, I was far too young.

I'd come to confession to tell the priest about the day, when a man who was following me asked if I wanted to earn a nickel. I thought he was going to put me to work when he took me to the third floor of an abandoned warehouse. I watched him as he walked around the dimly sunlit room, and peered out the window toward the busy harbor of the old seaport.

As my eyes adjusted to the light, I could see that the walls of this building were made of planks, caked with dust and cobwebs.

A musty odor filled the space, along with a few industrial contrap-
tions from livelihoods long passed. The ghostly silence of the
room echoed the screeches of hungry seagulls from the rooftops.

The man stood facing away from me for a short time. Then he
came and sat next to me on a wooden bench. Clasping my arm to
hold me still, he removed my swimsuit and forced me onto his lap
and touched me in ways no other grown-up had ever done. He
began ordering me to do things to him, and from the coarseness
of his voice, I thought he would hurt me, so I complied. The
downstairs door suddenly slammed, and I knew someone else had
entered the building. My molester was obviously startled, and he
bolted down the stairs. Another man approached from across the
room and scolded me for being in the place. I found my way out
and made it home.

When I got to my neighborhood, I told an older friend some
of what had just happened. He taunted me and spread the word
to everyone we knew. Whenever the issue surfaced, the response I
got was, "You shouldn't have let him do it," even before I got a
chance to explain exactly what had happened to me. After a
succession of similar remarks from authority figures in my life, I
internalized the idea that it was I who had done something so
wrong, that it set me apart from others.

The offense of that late summer afternoon and the unfortunate subsequent feedback I'd gotten, was what had led me to the
confessional. During the months it took me to get there, I believed
the black marks on my soul had possibly grown to the point of no
return.

After I told the priest my *easy* sins, he asked to hear the rest. I
continued by telling him about my childhood sexual explorations
with friends. He demanded to hear everything in detail.

"What else do you do?" he snapped.

I told him we liked looking at the pictures in the dirty books
we found.

The priest's reaction to this information made it increasingly difficult, if not impossible, for me to voice my darkest secret—the one I'd come to confess. Before I could even attempt to begin, the shadowy figure on the other side of the *screen-of-shame* manifested himself to be my worst possible nightmare and screamed at me at the untimeliest of moments.

"DO YOU REALIZE THE SERIOUSNESS OF WHAT YOU'VE DONE? YOU SHOULD BE WHIPPED!"

His scalding words betrayed my trust and usurped my desperate need for the validation I would never know.

I sat disoriented in the confessional, shocked right out of my body. The priest's anger and disgust toward me felt so intense, I nearly lost consciousness. I heard nothing else he said, except that I should go to the altar and say the penance he uttered. I walked down the aisle, consumed by guilt, believing that since I did not confess my worst sin, I was not forgiven, therefore, not acceptable to God. From the murmurs and quizzical expressions on the faces of the parishioners who were present in the church that night, there was no doubt that they'd heard the Father's livid ranting. They were probably wondering what on earth I could have done that was so terrible.

Upon my arrival at the altar, I had forgotten how many prayers of penance I was supposed to say. I simply knelt there for a long time, staring blankly at statues and stained-glass windows. I couldn't make it through even one, "Our Father..." As I headed home on that crisp clear night, I noticed that the sky was filled with stars, and that while walking beneath its midnight blue umbrella, I felt a comforting presence—a comfort I hadn't gotten from the priest.

The poison had been injected. There would be no cognitive therapy for symptoms associated with traumatic events, any time soon. But children are survivalists, and the things for which they have no remedy get tucked away inside them. Yet, those things are thoughts, and thought is energy. It doesn't just go away. Quite to the contrary, suppressed thought-energy compounds into patterns. I eventually learned that the suffering caused by repressed inner-conflict may be the thorn in our sides that spurs us to search for solutions, but in the interim, they can also cause us to fall prey to the detours of detrimental behaviors that lead to the destruction of the body.

The vision within a vision ended, and I heard Gloria say, "It wasn't your fault."

She leaned down to look directly at me, and added, "You must understand that you aren't to blame. You were never what the authority figures in your life thought you were, including the priest. Many, including me, were entangled in his web of error, and suffered the cruelty of his dominance."

Strength left me and my body went limp as I mouthed the words, "But he didn't hear what I came to confess."

"Your confession was meant to transform lies to truth. This couldn't happen through the priest, because the priest didn't know truth. His reaction was one of slander. But I do know truth, and I'm here to bear witness to the light of your soul."

I began to feel a little better at Gloria's comforting words.

"You went to the confessional, unaware that you would be offering up lies about your identity that were given to you. You accepted and believed them, but in reality, they had no place in you. The priest couldn't see this. The systems of thought ingrained in him were the illusory ideas, or lies, passed down to him by those who ruled him in *his* time of vulnerability. Be still now, and step aside from the false. In acknowledging a space between you and what is false, you become a *witness*, not a victim. The lamp of truth is now held high for you, so you can under-stand reality. Such recognition is the doorway of release from the clanging symbols of repetition, from delusion, and from the *sins of the fathers visited upon the children*. The vibration of the universe rises when just one soul is released through the recognition of truth. Every soul, and all of life, is exalted on this holiest of steps found along the pathway to the narrow gate."

My body was aglow in the light of Chief Great Blue Mountain's sudden transfiguration into the Archangel Gabriel. With royal-blue eyes, gazing out from an indescribable face resembling love manifested into form, he stood amid flickering beams of silver and indigo. He moved toward me with a fluidity I'd never seen, and then he bowed to me, and blessed my soul—an act I sensed deeply as the acknowledgment of the innocence of all God's children.

I felt thoroughly purged, and then I detected a new sensation around my eyes and mouth when, for the first time, ever, my adult face relaxed. I loved this feeling, and then I instantly realized what it was: I was comfortable in my own skin. I understood that Archangel Gabriel had heard my prayers and was the one who had set this entire rendezvous in motion, and that the crystal was a receptacle for his light-body, yet I sensed that in some mysterious way, the crystal was also a part of me. The purpose of the transfiguration was completed. When Great Blue Mountain reappeared, little did I know what awaited me.

Gloria became filled with an abundance of the living light which caused her aura to flicker while it cast a silvery-white corona around her head, and formed what I believed to be, a halo. She, too, had received healing at levels I was yet to know. Her vibration quickened, and immeasurable thankfulness rose from within me.

"You will grow now," she said. "Be patient—that's what time is for."

22

MESSAGE OF THE BUTTERFLY

"The most beautiful and most profound experience is the sensation of the mystical. It is the sower of all true science. He to whom this emotion is a stranger, who can no longer wonder and stand rapt in awe, is as good as dead."

— Albert Einstein

My body levitated, and I found myself being pulled upward by a magnetic current, and into the brilliance that shined from the crystal. As I stood, suspended in the all-encompassing vitality of its interior light, and in the throes of the Archangel Gabriel's frequency, I was filled with ecstasy throughout and beyond the cellular level of my being. If I were any closer to such a high frequency of vibration, I would likely have been incinerated.

While I hovered there, in awe of my heightened sense of oneness with everything, and of what it felt like to be alive in the moment, the intensity of the light subsided.

I watched as three leaves slipped through the air like feathers, and came to settle lightly, end-to-end, upon the serenity of what looked like a moonlit pond before me. When an insect lit gently upon the middle leaf, I became aware of a presence behind and to the left of me.

I gazed curiously at this small insect, and the benevolent entity whose presence I'd felt intermittently throughout my lifetime drew nearer. The great sense of relief instilled in me by this androgynous figure was tantamount to what a parent would feel upon the return of a lost child. As we watched this shiny, green and gold bug, I came to recognize it as a scarab. No explanation of the connection between the figure and I had yet come to light. The reason for its presence was kept aligned to a mysterious synchronicity, as were all thoughts pertaining to episodes in this alternate reality. Whatever entered my mind, did so, in its own time, without the force of my will.

As the scarab moved ever so slightly, the familiar soft hum of the universe caressed my ears, and I was enraptured by a blue-violet hue diffusing through the air. I had no thought concerning the *why* or *whereof*, when suddenly, the insect opened its shell in a burst of iridescence, and metamorphosed into a great and radiant butterfly with neon-like green wings with a pristine white perimeter receding into smaller sub-wings. This new dimension of life flared an aurora, far off into a mantle of darkness, and as its wings moved, ever so slowly in fan-like motion, I reveled in its bliss.

Questions and accusations regarding unpleasant situations from my past arose, but in the blink of an eye, I slipped into a state where those situations lost all import, like remnants of a senseless dream.

The loving figure who'd stood behind me during the metamorphosis of the butterfly, was now beside me. I sensed its guidance up to this point in my life. Exuberance flooded through me as we moved through a panorama of what I thought to be heaven. Void of pigmentation, the lush grass produced its own light, just as everything else I saw offered the softness of its own aura. Time had no place. The light scent of freshly cut melons caressed my nostrils as we traversed a pathway, lined with every kind of gemstone.

A temple that seemed to be made of frosted glass stood before me, but as I moved closer, I realized that it was made from the same substance as the Archangel Gabriel's light-body, only somewhat denser.

The distinct, ever-present hum of the universe continued to resonate in my ears as we made our way to the entrance. Without tactile sensation, we passed through a curtain of shimmering light, and upon entering, I noticed that I'd acquired a different kind of body—one that was weightless and composed of the fineness of blown glass.

The entire temple acted as a great prism, directing colored light throughout the farthest reaches of its form. I watched quietly as souls in this temple received healing infusions, emanated by a blend of colors. Earthly colors appeared flat in comparison to the vividness of these colors—each of which beautifully expressed its own key of sound from a celestial scale.

These souls had traveled from the physical dimension while their bodies slept. I gravitated toward one particular soul, and was astounded when I realized that it was Sandy, the young woman from The Gospel Lighthouse Church. Her distinctiveness had been invisible when I'd met her in the church. But seeing her in the multidimensionality of her soul was comparable to seeing all the colors, hidden in white light, cast into a rainbow. There was a fleeting moment when it was obvious that we were quite familiar with this overview of our lives. At her stage of growth in her earthly life, Sandy had needed to experience the power of belief. She'd done so when she'd internalized all the teachings of the church. The beliefs had overshadowed Sandy's life to the point where she thought she was standing at the gates of hell. She'd felt that she couldn't measure up to the ideals of the congregation that were based in their fearful scriptural interpretations. Her inability to sleep at night had brought on a nervous collapse. But she was at rest now and resonating with the wisdom of the ages with the help of the healing souls surrounding her.

Other areas of the temple presented different options for the progression of individual souls. I saw highly evolved souls, who had completed their cycles of incarnations into the physical plane, preparing to choose whatever realm would best serve the next phases in their evolution. I also noticed that the physical system was still a choice. Delighted at my investment of attention toward them, these souls enveloped me in the serenity of their gazes. The peace of avatars glowed on their faces and provided hints of what lay ahead for those who use time for its greatest purpose: to exude love. I was overwhelmed when they shared a glimpse into the next stage of their evolution with me. The love there was so amplified that even the word *love* itself could not do it justice. A fearful tremor passed through me as I stood there wondering why I had been so blind to such boundlessness. But then I recalled Gloria's instruction: *Don't look back.*

My benevolent friend then led me to an alcove in the temple where we sat in the rays of the reddest of reds, and found ourselves filled with all the shades of orange, yellow, green, blue, indigo, and violet. This particular progression had a fixed-velocity about it, and was accompanied by perfectly pitched tones rising in sync with each phase of color. Rivers of light calibrated every fiber of my form, and in a burst of whiteness, I was no longer separated from my friend. In fact, this androgynous figure turned into my likeness, and when I felt him shine from within me as the light of innocence, I discovered another dimension of *Amazing Grace*. To know color and sound in this way, and to realize that this figure was me, was one of the highest, exhilarating experiences of this journey, and of my life.

I found myself shifting away from the temple, moving slowly away from the interior light of the crystal, and back into the glory of the butterfly. Gloria came into view and appeared to be moving further into the light in the opposite direction. A thought that this loving soul's mission with me was nearing completion, surfaced in my mind. I understood her immeasurable reverence when a change in her facial expression captivated me while she pointed to my right.

"What is it Gloria? Where are you going?" I asked.

She smiled softly, nodded, and pointed again to where she wanted me to look.

I followed her direction, and uttered a deep gasp and a sigh of equal volume at what I saw. My breath caught in my throat when an area to my right *opened up* and my eyes fell upon my mother, who'd died years ago, standing in a blue-white field of brilliance. Ma was laughing and waving with glee, and she asked what took me so long to look.

The experience was a little too close to home, and when my heart became overloaded with unbearable excitement, Great Blue Mountain made a 180-degree sweep with his hand, and immediately quelled my hysteria.

My mother's light dimmed while she gazed lovingly at me, and said, "We didn't know about the series of events that happened to you as a child. Had we known, be assured, we would have protected you."

Amazingly, her brilliance returned after she reassured me that the past wouldn't matter, anymore.

"Look!" she said, gesturing toward her legs, "It's all gone now —the MS."

I felt an unfamiliar sensation inside my chest that seemed to open me up to breathing in a new way—a good way. As if in a daze, I reached into my shirt pocket to show my mother that I still carried the picture of Jesus she had given me on the day of my First Holy Communion.

"I know," she said, gently, "I know." She told me that every life had a purpose, and that there was a reason for our troubles that were actually jewels of life, meant to propel us to learn. She instructed me to adjust my focus and glance to an area beside her. I did as she suggested, and lo and behold, my big, Sicilian Grandmother appeared with my Grandfather in the same blaze of radiance. They reached out to embrace me, but I was quickly wrenched back by an invisible wave and didn't even have time to recognize the other souls who were with them.

Through a countenance of love, that only those who come near to divinity possess, Gloria shared that revelations of great truths happen at opportune times and, in accordance to a convergence of circumstances at magnitudes I couldn't yet know. I knew she was telling me that I couldn't stay attuned to these higher frequencies for too long because I was still entrained to the rhythms of the physical dimension.

I remembered the mystics' message regarding my Native American spirit guide's relevance to every color of the rainbow, and universal truths related to identity, belief, and perception, flashed through my mind's eye.

The space between Gloria and me increased gradually until, from afar, she appeared to blend with the sparkle of sunlight on the oceans of the world. She left me with the same solemn truth that came with the teachings of the mystics:

Remember to focus on the seed of truth growing within you in the face of opposition, for when you know truth, you will see there is nothing to fear.

With Gloria gone, the two stabilizing entities I had encountered on the stairwell parted in spirals of glitter. Chief Great Blue

Mountain remained and stood facing me, holding the magical crystal he'd created against his solar plexus.

He allowed the magnificence of its light to overcome and force me back with increasing velocity. I moved through what seemed a great distance, until the light shrank to a spot at the distal end of a long tunnel. Falling farther still, I was becoming accustomed to the feeling of gliding when I crashed into something with an abrupt thud. My heart was pounding so hard, I felt it in my throat. Unable to regain my bearings, I reached out to latch onto something—anything to give me some sense of grounding. Then I heard the sound of a baritone voice.

Looking up, shocked with astonishment, I found myself in the arms of Mrs. Marino, the voluminous Italian woman, who lived on the second floor of my home.

"Oh! Signore, are you okay?" She gasped. Her eyes shifted with askance, from me to a horde of oranges bouncing randomly down the stairs, and then back to me. She called frantically to her husband, "Dominic! Come here!"

I could only assume that she must have returned from the grocery store at the moment I was free-falling and had dropped her bags to prevent me from taking a backward tumble down the stairs.

Dominic arrived quickly, and after a rapid exchange of intense Italian language, they walked me to my room and brought me a glass of water. After I assured them that I was alright, they left to retrieve their groceries.

The clock on my bedroom wall read 10:30 a.m., which meant that only twenty-two minutes had passed since the time Jack brought me home and I'd entered through the front door. I was too disoriented to think about what had transpired in so short a time. Anyway, I wouldn't have had the space and solitude to devote to it at that moment since Mrs. Marino promptly returned with a bowl of chicken soup, a chunk of Italian bread, and some juice—just the nourishment I needed since I hadn't eaten break-fast at the hospital. I thanked her and as soon as she left, I indulged myself in her kindness.

After brushing my teeth, shaving, and taking a long, hot shower, I turned on the television. I didn't sit down to watch it, but as I shuffled around performing some light housework, the drone of commercials in the background provided a sense of balance after my heavenly soaring experience.

A two-week leave of absence from work came as a blessing. I spent most of the time in the woods refreshing my senses with nature. While absorbing my surroundings, I realized that many things had escaped me on previous excursions to the forest known as *Ravenswood.*

I felt a lightness in my being as I watched the limbs of tall oaks and maples bend in rhythm to the wind, and sunbeams flash-dance upon rustling leaves. I listened intently as birds of spring commenced their harmonious rituals, and the songs of the woods proclaimed the joy of new beginnings.

As I basked in the crispness of clarity, I wondered what had become of Sandy. Was she even real? Would I ever see Gloria, Great Blue Mountain, or the Archangel Gabriel again? I no longer had the crystal, nor had I ever shown it to anyone before my experience. There was nothing to verify that I had gone on this journey—nothing, nor anyone, except me. A fleeting thought crossed my mind regarding the possibility that through some mystical twist of fate, the experiences might have been all reflec-tions of my higher self.

I followed an upward-winding trail that eventually leveled off at its crest and spotted a massive rock to my right. Set between two oaks, it offered a spectacular vantage point overlooking the sea. I instinctively accepted its offer of repose and immediately noticed a rainbow gracing the expanse of the outer harbor. The rumble of thunder from a maritime squall faded, and I drifted beyond distraction and into the sound of silence.

And there, in the mindfulness of the moment, I forgave the world, and instantly felt free. Bliss rose from within, and as it surged upwards from the depths of my being, I knew that my life was forever changed.

QUOTE

"...While we don't look at the things which are seen, but at the things which are not seen. For the things which are seen are temporal, but the things which are not seen are eternal."

— 2 Corinthians 4:18

23

THE CONTINUING INTEGRATION

"Birth and death are not two different states, but they are different aspects of the same state. There is little reason to deplore the one, as there is to be pleased over the other."

— Mahatma Gandhi

Being away from work and not having to deal with much of anything in the world made my time of inner processing easier than if there had been demands placed upon me for things, which by then, I thought were unimportant. Whether I fished off the docks, hiked in the woods, bobbled with the motions of a moving train as I headed to explore the nooks and crannies of Boston, or just walked the city streets, my inner processing consistently ran in the background.

Practicing conscious intention was still a task while adjusting my focus to the instability of ever-changing objectivity. In the weeks to come, I knew there would be times when I'd get carried away by the shifting tides of opposition, but I also knew that my return to spiritual thinking would always be met with sameness—

not a boring monotony, but a welcome release from avenues of thought in which I tended to get lost.

In times of need, many of the truths that Gloria had shared with me surfaced in subtle ways like synchronous cogwheels. My life was to become a classroom for honing what she taught. While viewing complexity as limited and ego-based, I saw her lessons as simple. I had been conditioned to ego as my identity, which was simply a cluster of ideas about everything in life that hadn't completely gone away. But now, I had the ability to appraise my thoughts for what they were—or were not. The interim was the playing field for lubricating the scope of my perspective. I was in the midst of an integrative period where my Higher Self—the aspect of my being attuned to Spirit—brought messages of clarity to my lower self.

Shifting the poles of my identity from exclusive projection to all-inclusive vision was an ongoing rebirth. Mental stillness led to expansion. Like an antenna, repositioning itself to receive a signal, stillness opened to what I've learned, or have always known at the soul level.

Oscillating wasn't about being good, bad, right, or wrong, but about being conscious or unconscious. Having the qualities of a good person didn't mean that I was egoless, but instead that there are poles to ego, where being benevolent leaves us better off than being unkind. The truth to grasp here is that we don't *have* souls, but that we *are* souls, and as such, are infinitely larger than the context of the ordinary world's system of thinking.

God's Will is beyond my comprehension. I believe it's arrogant of the lower ego to assign its own definition to the Source of Life. In the case of mainstream religion, how could those who don't even control their own digestion think that they could preempt universal design with ideas of separation? But then again, as splinters of the Godhead, we have the power to project what we choose. Unfortunately, history proves, all too often, that we have chosen blindly.

The encapsulated ego-personality is incomplete, or *partial*, and can project nothing more than what it is. It can be likened to a fortress with inner walls made of mirrors as it staves off knowledge of universal wholeness. With the belief in death as its mainstay, the projecting ego perceives death everywhere. But its limited thinking has been exposed as counter to the truth, and its ideas of death, in turn, dead. Furthermore, the ego is a superiority complex that believes it is eternal, in some way; it's a belief it struggles to validate through forms of its religious dogmas. Versions of eternity are objectified and offered in mental constructs that lead to either life everlasting in heaven, or eternal death and separation from God, in hell. But as an interconnected whole, the universe has no such separation. The limited can never define the unlimited. We exist eternally, and though mindsets may be buried in cocoons of programming, the truth is that the residents of a dot in the Milky Way Galaxy can do nothing to change the ways of the universe.

Are so many people really afraid of death, or do they fear a loss of identity at relinquishing a hardened, false sense of their being? There has to be a point in the winds of time when humanity's unwillingness is softened by understanding, and then transformed into surrender at the deepest level.

Bible verses ran through my head, and I thought: *if only I could talk to Jack about all of this,* since he was so into the Bible. Even though I thought the Bible was one of the most metaphysical compilations ever put together, I found that it could be difficult to read and hard to understand. I thought that Jack would be resistant, except to the interpretations to which he was subjected. If there was fear directly related to one's God concept, it would be difficult for that person to appreciate the concepts I wanted to discuss.

I wouldn't become anyone's savior by forcing my views upon them, and it was important for me to accept that the universe had a way of taking care of itself. Just like everyone else, Jack needed to be where he was with his soul lessons, but since we once stood on common ground, I had a desire to share my point of view with him.

I'd hoped we could approach the subject material meekly, rather than with our individual needs to be right. I already felt justified within myself, so I had no need to seek anyone's approval; yet, I felt a void inside me for not having like-minded people to share it with. Despite my recent experiences, I knew that after a lifetime of cultural conditioning, forgetfulness was just a dream away. Truth was in me, but it took watering to sustain it. When it came to God, I was like a spiritual alcoholic who talked about the truth a lot, because I loved it.

My leave of absence was over and it was time to go back to the mundane, so I put my fishing pole and hiking boots away, for now.

I took a short cut through the woods on my way to work. As I walked, I breathed deeply and rhythmically because it helped me to relax before I had to enter the hubbub of the place. I now had such an interconnection with the outdoors, that I sometimes had strange thoughts about quitting my job and living in the woods. But my love for hot baths on cold winter nights quickly put a lid on that idea.

After the sublimity of the last two weeks, approaching the parking lot of my workplace felt like my final descent into the denseness of the material world. The moment I saw Jack's car bearing a *Jesus Saves* bumper sticker, I decided that I wouldn't be the one raising the topic of God. There was a high probability that he would assume the role of initiator, anyway.

I entered the building to Jack's announcement, "Here he comes, saved by the grace of God!"

"Hey Jack, how's it going? I guess we're all part of God's grace in one way or another, aye?"

"Are you ready to accept Jesus now, Sal? Another mishap like the last one might make your redemption impossible."

The familiar chasm between Jack and I was still there. In my mind, redemption was for empty cans and bottles. Had I not known about the *Unified Field Theory*, or what others would call Omnipresence, I would have felt only exclusion because I didn't fit into Jack's box. To him I was invisible—yet, I saw him, and all people as a part of me.

"But I do believe in Jesus, Jack. Whoever told you that I hadn't accepted Jesus?"

Memories of Jack's friends at his church flooded my mind, and I immediately became uncomfortable. The insidious air about them spoke of their belief in a God who kept score. I thought to myself, *I must walk my talk.*

"You aren't going to start with that New Age consciousness crap again, are you, Salvatore? That's what you were talking about in your sleep the night I stayed with you in the hospital after your accident. I couldn't stand to hear the words that were coming out of your mouth. I must warn you that Satan has a lot of tricks up his sleeve to keep you from the truth. All of that talk about other dimensions, reincarnation, and many lifetimes when we have only one life to live, comes from the enemy."

I recalled when the nurse had told me that she had heard Jack and I conversing that night in the hospital, when I knew for a fact that I had been asleep at the time. My interdimensional experience must have overflowed into the words I apparently spoke while in deep sleep. Now I understood why Jack had acted so strangely in the car while driving me home from the hospital that day.

"I agree that there is only one life, Jack, although different from the way you see it. Whether or not reincarnation exists,

REFLECTIONS OF MY HIGHER SELF

doesn't change that fact. However, just to be clear, I do believe in it. Reincarnation, that is."

I also believed that Jesus was a misunderstood teacher, and that it was against universal law and, therefore impossible, for anyone to learn your evolution *for* you. *Anyone*, included Jesus. All life energy is a continuum—All One Life. In keeping with this truth, I believed we had many lifetimes within LIFE to accomplish what could not be done in the span of one lifetime.

"I hope you don't expect me to ever believe in reincarnation, Salvatore. There are false prophets all over the place laying snares to snatch our souls away from God. Narrow is the gate, and Jesus is the way to salvation."

"Can you explain what you mean by that, Jack?" I asked, already knowing that he couldn't in its truest form.

"It doesn't need explanation; it's a mystery. You only have to believe that Jesus died for you and washed your sins away through his suffering. You must plead the sacrificial blood of the Lamb of God as an offering from his Father for your salvation and rightful inheritance. God so loved the world that he gave his only begotten son so you might be saved."

"Jack, I'm not against you. I believe everything you believe, just from a different angle. In your interpretation of Bible scripture, you believe in separation and death. I don't hold that belief. But I don't condemn you for doing so."

"You have to be either hot or cold in the Lord, Salvatore. There's no lukewarm. You cannot serve two masters. The Word is The Word, and God will not be mocked."

"I agree, Jack."

I heard a voice in my head warn, *All shields up!* Since so much of my past had been grievously affected by Jack's type of belief system, it was imperative that I stood, consciously, in the light of what was true for me in the moment.

"How do you agree, Salvatore?"

"I believe it means we either see things the way they are, or we don't. A person cannot mock what they don't know, and in this case, if they did know, they wouldn't mock. You hold to beliefs of eternal separation from God. That's where we disagree about basics like Omnipresence and Absolute Reality. I don't damn you because of your beliefs. I see you as an extension of God, regardless of your beliefs."

I didn't want to preach to Jack, nor try to save him from his scary thoughts, unless he asked me to, in some direct way, which he hadn't. Had he asked, I would have had to approach the subject under different and special circumstances. I enjoyed sharing my thoughts with people who were open and interested when the subject was up for discussion. To offer my beliefs to someone whose only intent was to try to invalidate them, was a needless drain on my energy.

Jesus spoke metaphorically during *The Sermon on the Mount*. I wanted to share study about that with Jack, particularly the metaphor about taking the log out of your own eye before trying to remove the speck from your brother's eye. It was a clear representation of projection. But if Jack ever felt drawn to take a serious look at the laws of belief and perception, he would be led to do so and, probably without my help. People tend to place confidence in strangers and seek advice from the inhabitants of far-off lands before listening to their neighbors, whose past folly they've likely witnessed and remember.

There is a fine line between being helpful and being invasive to someone's personal boundaries. Boundaries are to be respected, and I found myself getting a little too close to Jack's. Once again, I had to take a humbler approach to life, and to the people around me. An important lesson to realize is that when the student is ready, the teacher would appear. Everyone was where he or she needed to be in order to learn and attain a higher understanding of all our places in a greater purpose.

Part of my learning was to lay low, and to give a longer period of incubation to what I had found to be real, so it could take root and grow. If there was a time for me to yell my truth from the rooftops, this surely wasn't it.

In reflecting later that day, it was obvious to me that I was feeling somewhat upset about Jack's resistance. But was this truly the case, or was I upset because I felt the need to control Jack? If the later was the case, then I'd have to ask myself why I needed Jack's agreement or his approval, which would actually be a form of idolization. The old cliché: *what goes around comes around,* is true, and that day, it hit me square in my face. Humility was the lesson that would continue to return until I learned it. Lessons seemed to come quickly, lately. The lesson here regarding Jack, was that there are times when even the closest friends may choose to part, hopefully temporarily, and in peace.

I loved the feel of Ravenswood, and I returned the following weekend to walk its dirt trails again. I was awed by the flood of thoughts that came to mind during times of reflection beneath its canopy of treetops. The difference between real vision and my ordinary way of looking at things became evident again. Answers came quickly while in this receptive state, sometimes even before I completed the questions in my mind.

While thinking about the turmoil in the world and, telling myself that I was above it in some way, I realized that becoming what people commonly call *spiritual* wasn't a ticket out of the world, but rather about learning to appraise the world differently. It was important to be a viable, contributing force in the community.

Although the world reflected the meaning I placed upon it through my organic senses, and the overlay of conditioning ingrained in me, I received intangible insights about what lay beneath such appearances, while taking these walks. I came to see all of life as the Son of God.

To perceive from a place beyond my projections meant that I could extend a pureness of thought through me, and toward others—not because I was special, but because the way had been cleared for a fact of life that's available to everyone. A higher reality is at everyone's core, and it cannot be affected by anything. Old, habitual thinking stirred, but I made the decision to listen to the corrections in quiet ways. In moments of despair, my inner voice became clear and assured me that the door of reformation is never closed.

Gloria's explanation of an integrative period was making sense. Thoughts of a higher octave of vibration were infusing my overall psychology in accordance to my focus. Was I ready to make the leap from mostly conceptualizing these truths, to experiencing their application to my daily life? The immediate answer from inside me was: *I hope so, or what else was all this for?*

Once again, I could see the difference between discerning vision and my ordinary way of looking at things. The latter resembled a self-contained unit stirring its sameness. The thought rose in me to continue to loosen encapsulated thinking regarding identity, and to watch the light of infinity shine away faulty ideas of pseudo self-righteousness. The thought lifted me, reinforcing my belief that we are so much more than what we know.

24

THE EYE OF THE SOUL

"All you can learn is what your inward life is and try to stay loyal to that."

—Joseph Campbell

I wanted to find my friend, Michael. He had a way of assisting me with keeping my feet planted on the ground. As I walked into town, I felt light as a feather even while thunder clashed overhead, lightning cracked the sky, and heavy downpours had me ducking into doorways. I was drenched, but I relished every moment of it.

Michael had once told me that he performed chakra cleansing, so I hoped he would show me his method. My mystical mentors had begun to teach me how to clear myself of mental poison, along with other ways of self-protection. But I was still open to learning. In that sense, I looked forward to meeting with Michael.

I peeked through a plate-glass window of the neighborhood grocery store, and saw Tony, the owner, and his daughters, Pam and Gina. I'd known them for many years, back when I worked as a delivery man, so I stopped in to say hello, and to buy something to drink for my upcoming walk on the beach.

"Salvatore!" Tony uttered in a loud cry, "You're drenched. The towels are out back. You know where to find the bathroom. How have you been?" Tony's perpetual smile radiated from his face. He'd always made it known that he was glad to see me.

"I'm doing great, Tony. How about you? You're looking good!"

"Yeah, baby! Everything is beautiful. What makes the difference is how we look at things—our attitude. You know that, right, kid?"

"Yep, Tony, you know I do."

"Thatta boy, Salvatore," he said, and then stepped aside to help a clerk who was having issues with a customer's credit card payment.

Pam and Gina were all smiles. This family was always warm and welcoming. My chest tingled whenever I was around them. I wished there were more people like them in my life. I asked the girls if they'd seen Michael.

They said they weren't sure they knew who Michael was, which surprised me, since I'm certain Michael had been in the store with me on numerous occasions.

Going lone-wolf and moving to the west side of the island last year, had brought excitement with novel things to do and see. I had felt a sense of freedom while settling into my new abode with its spectacular view of the ocean that I loved. But on the other hand, there were more people here than there were in East Gloucester. Without fail, there were always customers ahead of me with issues—be it coupons, cash, check, or charge, and I wasn't looking forward to standing in line at the grocery store today.

The man in front of me dropped his wallet. It didn't take long for the stink of cigarettes and stale beer to permeate the air when he stooped to retrieve it. A host of other aromatic emissions rose from the unseasonably heavy sweater and faded blue jeans he was wearing. The foliage entangled in the laces of his antiquated Reeboks set off a chain of image-laden thoughts in me about the burdens of the homeless. *There I go, but for the grace of God,* I thought, as he reinserted the box of rolling tobacco that had escaped his pants' pocket in his rush to log-arm a twelve-pack of brew.

I eyed him as he carefully meandered his way across the wet floor toward the door. Before he opened it, he turned and thanked the clerk in a rasping voice. Then he looked directly at me, smiled shyly, winked his gray-blue eyes, and said, "Your shapeshifting friend is at the music store."

I nipped my judgmental attitude in the bud and stared at him from the place within that went beyond appearances. He finally turned and stepped outside into the calm after the storm. With no recollection of ever meeting him, I figured he must have heard me ask the girls if they'd seen Michael. I thought that everyone knew Michael, but I had no idea what the guy meant by calling him a shapeshifter. Was he referring to Michael's fluctuating weight? I didn't know, so I blew it off for the moment.

With a hasty goodbye to Tony and the girls, I left the grocery store and headed down the street toward the music store. I came face-to-face with Michael as he emerged from the side door of the building.

"Salvatore! Where have you been? I heard you got hurt at work. I've come knocking several times, but you haven't answered your door. What the heck happened to you? Are you alright?" Michael shrieked, in a disconcerting manner.

I appreciated his concern, yet was startled by his awkward overemphasizing.

"Yeah, I'm doing alright, Michael. I had a bizarre experience. It's a long story. I'll tell you about it, eventually. It's something like the mystical dream you once told me you had. That kind of thing," I added, knowing that Michael was the one person who could relate to my spiritual journey into self.

"Well, I'm sure glad to hear you're alright, kid," he replied more calmly.

"Thanks," I said. "So, you can stop worrying about me now, okay?"

"Ah, yes, okay yes." Michael acquiesced. "You still remember me telling you about my dream, do you? My dream wasn't like any other dreams I've had. It was real."

"In some ways, they are Michael, they are."

Michael peered at me, appraising my responses with unusual focus. Without assigning any particular significance to his pause, I let it pass quickly along with the rest of his strange glibness.

"So, what happened to you at work? What was it— three weeks ago?"

"Aw, Michael, now isn't the time, but I'll fill you in later. I'm alright. The episode just brought me to a place of major intro-spection. Right now, I don't want to think too much. I just want to thoroughly enjoy the beach before sunset. But it's a drag that I left my freaking water at the store."

"Well, you were born to think. Not the common man that's for sure. Sometimes I see smoke coming out your ears," Michael said with a grin.

"Look closely now and you might see rainbows," I said, jokingly. "Seriously though, will you show me how you do the healing thing you do?"

"You mean chakra cleansing?" he asked, knitting his brows together.

"Yeah— the one where you use your hands."

Michael led the way from the door of the music store to an area on the sidewalk that wasn't so crowded. I figured it was in reaction to passers-by staring at us with puzzled looks on their faces.

He cleared his throat before speaking. "All I do is acknowledge myself as a clear and open channel for universal forces that heal, and then I direct energy to the chakras. I use visualization and breath, and sometimes sound. It depends on how I want the energy to flow."

"You can direct how the energy flows?"

"Uh, huh. It's not so complicated. I just do what comes to mind. There's no strict protocol to it, except that you need to feel compassion while doing it. You can call it healing energy, but it's actually the frequency of universal love. I feel my way through the process without getting in the way, so to speak."

"I've channeled healing energy before, naturally, when I had no set method."

"Yeah, well— that's because it is natural. Are you referring to the time with your mom?" he asked, staring at me intently.

"Yes, and she definitely received healing," I replied on a puzzled frown. The part of my brain that dealt with memory always worked like a charm. I didn't recall telling Michael anything about the healing experience with my mom or, in fact, ever mentioning her to him at all.

"Healing is always received, Salvatore," he added quickly, as if to deter me from asking how he knew about my mother. "But it's not always as obvious as we wish it to be. If it served their highest good, a person could even die after receiving healing. It's not about getting the visible results we want every time. We don't always see the whole picture. But the energy always goes to some level of the person's being, while a person's being goes beyond their body."

Michael gestured for us to commence our usual walk. The sky cleared as we headed toward the beach, and dusk made way for an early star that hung like a lantern in the east. Salt from the ocean, mingled with mild breezes leftover from the squall soothed my senses.

"It's a breath of fresh air to see you, Michael, but slow down. Are you going to a fire or something?" I asked as he hopped from one foot to another while glancing around warily.

"I just want to get away from the tourists and the looky-loos— be in my own territory— my section of the beach. Let's go over to *that* rock where we can sit comfortably."

In the seriousness of the moment, I came close to breaking the silence with laughter at the thought that Michael seemed to believe he owned a section of the beach, just because he'd made that allusion so often. He stepped behind me and placed his hands on my shoulders. "Hot dang! Salvatore, your energy is amazingly clean. What have you been doing?"

"I promise to tell you later. Just keep going with the healing process. As long as I'm not going to die, to somehow serve my greater good!" I said halfheartedly. I wanted to use my healing method in concert with his. I'd felt that our energies would act synergistically, and they did the moment he put his hands on my shoulders.

"I wouldn't worry about dying today. Not with this type of healing exercise." Michael said while laughing. "Maybe you shouldn't be so afraid of death, anyway," he offered on a more serious note.

"Okay, I'll give it my best shot," I responded, with a roll of my eyes.

He squeezed my shoulders. "There's a high feeling on the beach today, Salvatore. Do you feel it?"

Stopping short of proposing that it emanated from us, I kept my mouth shut.

Michael added that the energy was from the attitude of everyone on the beach, and then he proceeded to move his hands upward from my shoulders to my crown chakra at the top of my head. He made his way to my third eye, my throat, my heart, my solar plexus, and finally to my creative and ground chakras.

When he was done with the laying on of his hands, Michael remarked that he'd seen the colors of my chakras, and that he'd heard a tone coming from each one. After my experiences of late, this didn't surprise me. I silently reciprocated his compassion and directed healing energy to him in the same manner he'd directed his to me. But when I touched him during the healing process, I noticed that I felt tremendous heat coming from his chakras.

The sun was slipping in a blaze of magnificence beneath the horizon as we continued to walk the beach. I felt as though the ocean breeze was blowing right through me, and that I'd grown a foot taller. I had experienced this feeling on numerous, previous occasions— once at a local temple service I'd attended with Michael, where the monk at the podium had commented on a *feeling in the room.*

I wanted to talk to Michael about his version of the ego, but I refrained, and elected to let the conversation flow. At times like this, he usually picked up on my cerebral calisthenics without me saying a word. Sure enough, he brought up a similar topic that I knew would lead directly to what I wanted to discuss.

"Your crown chakra has such a beautiful energy flowing through it, and your spiritual eye has been opened recently. I can tell, because it's quite warm. What did you do, Salvatore? Have you been soul-searching or meditating a lot? Are you looking at things differently these days, or what?"

"Since you mentioned it— yes. I've been looking at the differ-ence between my sleeping self and my more awakened outlook. My mind did a sort of shift, like the turning of a kaleidoscope. It's like everything looks different, yet all the same parts are still there."

"Ah, Salvatore, so you went through some turnabouts? Hooked up with Universal Mind, did you?" he said with genuine excitement and spiritual camaraderie. "You'll go through more changes, but you'll get the knack of it. A bit disorienting at first, huh?" His smile was encouraging.

"To say the least, Michael. To say the least." I felt like my heart would burst at the simplicity of sharing my experience with someone who understood.

"Just go with it, Salvatore, and remember that a period of feeling somewhat disoriented is a part of the process. People can feel strange when their underpinnings are being renovated, you know. It's a transitional phase of re-identification."

He dipped his head and peered at me. "Do you feel more grounded every day, and are things looking brighter? Have you unloaded a lot of excess baggage?" He chuckled. "Take a look in the mirror tonight. You might find that you glow in the dark."

"Ha, ha! Not glowing yet, but I do feel much lighter, Michael. Situations from the past tend to lurk in the background and come to haunt me now and then, but they've lost power over me. There's a change happening inside. And it's a good one."

"You won't be haunted by the past much longer. The past is like smoke in the wind. Heck, it doesn't even exist, except as a memory trace. Just focus on the broader perspective you escalate to, and you'll equalize on a higher plateau. That's all you really want right now, you know. You don't have to grasp everything under the heavens with your chronological mind."

I silently welcomed all his advice, since I knew that it would come in handy sometime in the future, as I worked to get a handle on things.

"*Life is about being,* Salvatore. For now, it's enough to come out of the wilderness. The part of your mind that you're tapping into is complete. It doesn't really expand. You're only opening to what's already there; you just have a clearer lens to look through now."

I stopped short in my tracks and turned to look him in the eye. "Hey! How did you know that, Michael? I mean— where did you hear *life is about being?* Do you know Gloria? I've never spoken to you about what happened to me, or where I heard those exact words! And by the way, you still haven't said anything about what you found on the beach that night. What was it that washed from the ancient Native bottomlands and into the sea, and then dredged and deposited onto the beach? Michael! Was it a crystal?"

A wave of shock shot through me as I began to wonder if Michael was yet another reflection of my higher self, just as I had been wondering about Gloria, Great Blue Mountain, and the Archangel Gabriel. But Michael had always appeared to me in this world of form, not in an alternate reality. Yet, I couldn't understand why his face had appeared during Great Blue Mountain's transfiguration into the Archangel Gabriel, as he'd stood in the pillar of light on my stairwell landing. Were they all the same person?

My heart began to throb when it finally dawned on me that no one had ever acknowledged Michael's presence when he was with me. Even though Michael had accompanied me to the store several times in the past, Pam and Gina didn't know who he was when I'd enquired about him earlier today. Apparently, no one even knew him! Except, of course, for the homeless guy at Tony's neighborhood grocery store. But that guy had referred to Michael as a shapeshifter. Was the homeless guy privy to some ability Michael had to morph into different bodies? Either that, or there was much more to the homeless guy than what I had seen. Of course there was, I thought with a shake of my head. During my journey it had been made very clear to me that there was more to everyone.

It was becoming uncomfortably clear to me that Michael was invisible to others, and I was beginning to think he had the ability to take on the physical appearance and personality of other beings.

I wondered now about the patrons' behavior in the bar on the night of Michael's return from Montana. No wonder they were pointing and laughing at me. I must have appeared like a raving lunatic interacting with someone they couldn't see. Adding to that conundrum was the fact that I'd overlooked his familiarity and knowledge about people from my past, and of things about my life that he shouldn't have known—like my mother's healing he'd mentioned earlier. As we stood there by the ocean, I peacefully accepted the continuing enigma of Michael. He was a wholesome mystery, since all he'd ever done was not only teach me how to look out for myself, but also how to find my true self.

I realized that he still hadn't responded to my question about whether or not he'd found a crystal the night we walked the beach. But as I thought about it, I realized that if he did have a direct association with the crystal, then it would mean he was, indeed, Great Blue Mountain, my Spirit Guide, the one who'd created the crystal, and who was its caretaker. Gloria had told me that he had the power to draw the crystal to himself. That could be what Michael had done when he'd found the mysterious object at the pipe's outlet that night. But how did Gloria come to possess the crystal, unless Great Blue Mountain had given it to her?

I was overcome with the idea that each of the three, and the journey itself, were all one expression of my Higher Self talking to *me*. Or perhaps they'd communicated with my lower self as I'd lain on the floor of my workplace, unconscious to the everyday world, and then later in the hospital, and also on the stairwell of the Victorian I called home. Could this really be what had happened? One thing I did know, was that everything I experienced seemed as real as the everyday world. Would these questions be answered? Could I be losing my sanity?

I recalled that, not long ago, I came to believe that *what we think to be dreams may very well be realities.* My belief stemmed from the fact that when I had awakened from my accident, I still had the crystal Gloria had placed in my hand! Could the crystal have been an injury-related hallucination? I think not.

As Michael and I continued to walk in silence, thoughts that defined Omnipresence began to surface in me in a strange but gentle way. These thoughts were mathematical, and demonstrated how we are all ONE as *aspects* of a Universal Soul. This meant that in the world of form, we live in the perspective of duality where we perceive a separate *you and me.* But it also meant that at the core of being, there is the perspective of singularity, where *you and me* are not seen as separate, but *known* as ONE. There was a grace to these thoughts that flowed through me like a cleansing wind song.

I was parched, and I thought how satisfying it would be to quench my thirst with the bottle of sparkling water I'd unintentionally left at Tony's store. My yearning activated my imagination to the point where I saw the bottle in my mind's eye. I visualized myself tasting it and feeling the sensation of drinking it. To my great surprise, a bottle of sparkling water appeared in my hand! I whipped my head around to see if there was anyone who could have placed it there, but there was only Michael and, he wasn't close enough to me to have done it.

My feet had become sore from this arduous walk on the sand, and I thought how much better they'd feel had I been a little lighter. Wouldn't you know, I became lighter and my feet became happier! I was manifesting spontaneously. Did this mean I had grown to be a self-actualizing God-Man? The paradox here was that the degree of gratification I basked in with this new ability to create wasn't new to me. It felt strangely familiar. I couldn't pinpoint exactly when or where, but I was certain that I'd known this *Emmanuel State* before. And then, suddenly, every sensory apparatus within me revealed the potential I had to fulfill every one of my benevolent wishes. I was awe struck.

Immediately, I began to notice a soft white light surrounding everything in sight. At first, this light made me wonder if there was something wrong with my vision, but I knew there wasn't when the light soothed my entire body and state of mind. *Luxurious*, was a fair description of what I was experiencing. There was a subtlety to this fine light as it increased to where I could see and feel it scintillating in the sand and all around and through me. Then came the low *hum of the universe* with which I was so familiar.

Light and Sound! These were the two Principles of Creation that Gloria had said would come to remind and assure me that I was never alone.

Michael looked north to where the river flowed from the bottomlands into the sea. He wasn't one to speak until he was ready, so I remained patient for his long-awaited answer. I was puzzled when he uttered the kind of chuckle that indicated one was hiding a secret, but I hung onto his every word when at last he spoke.

"You arrive at a place of recognition when you use mental alchemy by focusing on the seed of truth growing within you rather than on the unfortunate and distracting experiences in life. It has nothing to do with a distant God, but of who you are, here and now, as you awaken to the simplicity of being. No longer, then, will you view life as though through a dark glass.

"I am always with you, Salvatore. Even when you flounder on the surface of life. In your heart, you already know that you have come closer to home, to a higher reality, so allow for this recognition to take place and then accept it thoroughly. Let go and surrender at last! For in this, you are coming to remember you. When you come to fully know you, not only will you know me, but you will know everyone, and then what you call *God* will do the rest while the frequency of The Milky Way Galaxy

REFLECTIONS OF MY HIGHER SELF

continues to quicken as it moves into another sector of the cosmos."

I sat down on the beach, picked up a handful of sand, and sifted it through my fingers as I realized that I wasn't too shocked by Michael's indirect, yet encompassing answer, because, by this point, my old mind was already seriously shaken and pretty much blown. He had told me that night at the bar that he was a Black-foot Indian, and according to the mystery school, my spirit guide was also a Blackfoot. What was even more jolting was that he'd taken what he'd found that night on the beach to Montana for a holy cleansing ceremony. What could it have been other than the crystal? I had theorized that Michael was, indeed, Great Blue Mountain, but now, in light of so many interwoven circumstances, it seemed to be progressing to fact.

At her first intercession with me, Sister Clementus had placed the crystal in my hand. Was this Michael's way of showing it to me in a very big way? I felt I knew deep down who he was, who all of them were. I recalled the metamorphosis of the butterfly and its profound symbolism of the greatest change anyone could ever undergo. Then I thought about the androgynous figure who'd walked with me to the temple of light during the metamor-phosis. I knew that this figure, this person, had been with me throughout my life, which proved true, when, ultimately, the figure had shone from within me as the light of innocence. The way I felt about this figure was the same way I felt about Gloria, Great Blue Mountain, the Archangel Gabriel, and now, about Michael, and even about the crystal. Were they all different versions of the same thing? A higher part of my being? In that moment on the beach, I felt as if I was walking toward the temple of light again.

It was difficult for me to wrap my mind around the idea that my journey, the beautiful crystal, and all the people involved might have been reflections of my own inner light, my Higher Self. So rather than over-think it, I let it be. I also found that even though they had shown me so many things, they couldn't just put answers into my head *for* me. No one can ever give anyone answers about the mysteries of the universe. My journey, and everything about it, presented me with understanding. It was required of me to apply the understanding to allow answers, or states of being to arise from within my own consciousness accordingly.

Questions still loomed in my analytical mind regarding my mystical odyssey, particularly where Michael and the crystal were concerned. But even more increasingly now, moment-to-moment, my questions seemed to simultaneously present solutions, to the point where there was no longer anything left to ask. I wanted to share this new ability with Michael. He was the expression of life closest to me in the physical world of form, and I had actually grown to love him.

Before I could turn enough to face my friend in this vastly open space, my mind illuminated with thoughts of the androgynous figure who had become the light of innocence within me. Moving ever so slowly, I completed my turn to face him.

In that moment, I instantly knew everything, and I understood why: Michael was gone.

EPILOGUE

I knew I had a tale to tell that depicted my life experiences, but I didn't sit with the intention of writing it. What began as a five-hundred-word short story took on a life of its own. I felt pushed out of the way when a movie in my head took control. My only task was to write the words to describe what I was seeing.

Although there was no accident at my workplace, no appearance of the translucent woman, and no existence of the crystalline gemstone in the external world of form, most of the occurrences in this book are true to a startling degree in that they are actual reflections of my higher self.

Divinity is a word used to describe the incorruptible part of everyone at the core of their being. It's there to be acknowledged, rather than acquired. More than a free gift, it simply *is*. To realize this and extend our divinity to the divinity of others—even through a silent thought—is what I believe to be our larger purpose in the world. A purpose that, when accomplished, will lift us out of the repetitive movie of our interpretations of birth, life, and death.

As a work in progress, I still learn to appreciate personal hardships as stepping-stones. Yet, I've come to know seeds of change aren't only sown in misfortune, but also in the joy of removing the many coats we wear, one-by-one. I'm grateful for coming to recognize my life as a blessed journey, into which I've barely taken a single step.

ABOUT THE AUTHOR

Joseph Danna is an Advanced Bodyworker and an Initiate of The Rosicrucian Order, AMORC. He owns and operates a pain relief and relaxation clinic in New England, where he lives. He accepts his insights as aspirations in a simple way. His other book is titled, "From Smoking & Vaping to Breathing", in which Joe explains how he used the natural laws of the universe to end his tobacco-dependency habit.